Trout Streams
of Virginia

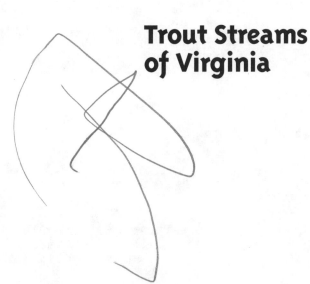

The author fishes a plunge pool in the Alleghany Highlands.

Trout Streams of Virginia

Harry Slone

An Angler's Guide to the
Blue Ridge Watershed

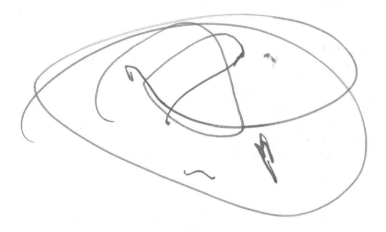

3RD EDITION

Backcountry Guides
Woodstock, Vermont

An Invitation to the Reader

With time, access points may change, and road numbers, signs, and landmarks referred to in this book may be altered. If you find that such changes have occurred near streams described in this book, please let the author and publisher know so that corrections can be made in future editions. Other comments and suggestions are also welcome. Address all correspondence to:

Fishing Editor
Backcountry Guides
P.O. Box 748
Woodstock, VT 05091

Library of Congress Cataloging-in-Publication Data

Trout streams of Virginia: an Angler's guide to the Blue Ridge watershed / Harry Slone. — 3rd ed.

        p.   cm.

   Rev. ed. of: Virginia trout streams. 2nd ed., rev. and expanded. 1994.

    ISBN 0-88150-472-6 (pbk. : alk. paper)

    1. Trout fishing–Virginia. I. Slone, Harry, 1929– Virginia trout streams. II. Title.

SH688.U6S56 1999

799.1'755–dc21   99–28589

                                                CIP

© 1991, 1994, 1999 by Harry Slone

Third Edition

Published by Backcountry Guides, a division of The Countryman Press, P.O. Box 748, Woodstock, VT 05091

Distributed by W. W. Norton & Company, Inc., 500 Fifth Avenue, New York, NY 10110

Cover and text design by Joanna Bodenweber
Cover photograph by Brooks Dodge/New England Stock Photo
Interior photographs by Kenneth F. Norton, Harry Steeves, Stephen Hiner, and Harry Slone
Maps by Richard Widhu © 1991, 1994, 1999 The Countryman Press; Chapter 9 map by Mapping Specialists Ltd., Madison, WI

Printed in the United States of America

10 9 8 7 6 5 4 3

ACKNOWLEDGMENTS

The author is happy to acknowledge individuals who helped in the preparation of *Trout Streams of Virginia:* Larry Mohn, Virginia fisheries biologist, regional manager; Mark Hudy, head biologist, National Park Headquarters in Washington; Stephen Hiner, aquatic entomologist, Virginia Polytechnic Institute; Tim Trevilian, photographer and maker of custom graphite rods; photographers Kenneth Norton, Norm Willis, Bob Leonard, Sandy Hevener, Richard Smith, Lloyd Campbell, and Katharyn Douglass Hopkins; and Mike Peters, tireless fishing partner.

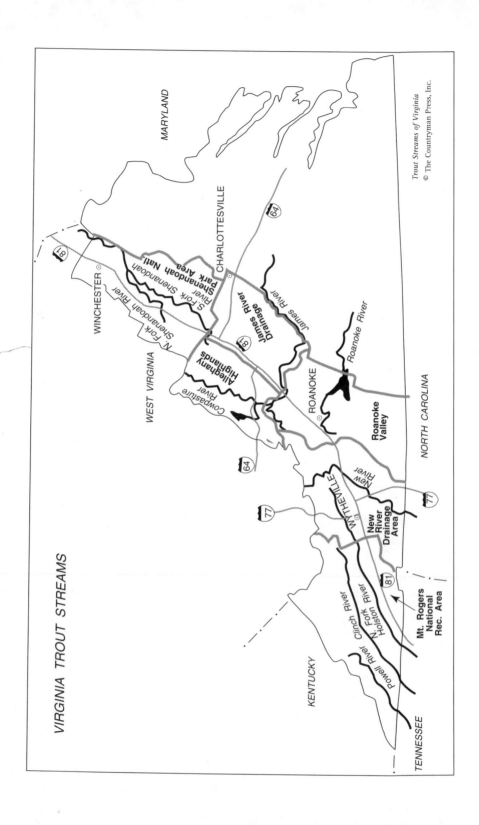

VIRGINIA TROUT STREAMS

MARYLAND

WEST VIRGINIA

WINCHESTER ⊙

N. Fork Shenandoah River

S. Fork Shenandoah River

Shenandoah Natl. Park Area

CHARLOTTESVILLE ⊙

James River Drainage

James River

Allegheny Highlands

Cowpasture River

ROANOKE ⊙

Roanoke River

Roanoke Valley

NORTH CAROLINA

KENTUCKY

Powell River

Clinch River

N. Fork Holston River

Fork River

WYTHEVILLE ⊙

New River

New River Drainage Area

Mt. Rogers National Rec. Area

TENNESSEE

Trout Streams of Virginia
© The Countryman Press, Inc.

Contents

PREFACE TO THE THIRD EDITION

In writing the first edition of *Trout Streams of Virginia* (originally titled *Virginia Trout Streams*), I had a clear-cut objective. No really comprehensive guide existed for fly-fishermen and -women who wished to explore the trout possibilities in Virginia, and I wished to fill that gap. I have to say that the very positive response to the book indicates that it fulfilled its objective. Moreover, during its writing I met some remarkable people, made a lot of new friends, and had some highly rewarding conversations with many of my readers.

Recently I spoke with a knowledgeable guide to Virginia, Patagonia, and points west. He lectures around the country and begins each presentation with, "If you fly-fish in Virginia, you'll need three things: a catch-and-release net, the DeLorme Gazetteer, and Harry Slone's book, *Trout Streams of Virginia*!" Over the years the many responses like this have been my true reward, and music to my ears!

There were two other major reasons for writing this third edition. Since I made the last revisions to *Trout Streams of Virginia* in 1996, there have been many changes to the state's trout program. And independent of the Virginia Game and Inland Fisheries projects, private pay-for-fish streams here have mushroomed. In previous editions there was only one such stream listed, the Cascades at the Homestead. Now seven more have been added, some of them charging as much as $50 per rod for a day's fishing—and they're booked solid.

Most, but not all, of these privately run operations are fly-fishing only, catch-and-release. Only a limited number of anglers are allowed on the stream on a given day. What this adds up to is a quality fishing experience, with plenty of elbow room, and sometimes even solitude. There aren't hordes crowding onto the honey holes, there's no traffic along the road cruising for pods of stocked fish, and no caravan of pickups following the stocking truck. It's an opportunity to see nature at its best without a blight of Styrofoam worm cups and Mello Yello cans.

Pay-for-fish is not for everyone, but for someone willing to pay it fills a vacuum. The thrill of hooking really big fish, of having a 5-pound rainbow bend your 5-weight rod double, even the pop of a 4X leader parting—these experiences make private fishing worthwhile. This aspect of Virginia trout fishing is growing, and no doubt there will soon be many more in addition to the eight streams I have included in this third edition. Not all of the locations I fished rewarded me with an authentic day of fly-fishing. They may be added to later revisions, as their operations develop. But for now it is my earnest hope that readers will explore this new world of pay-for-fish trout streams and come away arm-weary at the end of the day.

Mapping and fishing Virginia's trout waters brought me to many enjoyable places, but always in the back of my mind was one memorable stream, the Big Laurel. It did not appear in my first edition and it isn't in the second for one simple reason: I never was able to find it. In fact the Big Laurel has been lost to me since the year 1946.

That was a joyful year for Americans, with the ending of World War II and the beginning of postwar optimism. In my little high school in Salem, Virginia, there was a new presence. Those students who had volunteered their services during their senior year, or earlier, had climbed out of their foxholes and gun tubs, tossed their duffel bags into Salem's attics, and gone back to school. These were men, but there they were sitting behind their childhood desks, studying history and civics for the sake of obtaining a diploma.

Imagine my pride when a group of those veterans invited me to go trout fishing with them, while I was only a fresh-faced high school junior. One May morning in 1946 we pulled out at 4 AM and headed for a stream my companions called the Big Laurel. A couple of hours later we parked on the side of a dirt road high in the mountains, just as the first streaks of dawn redness hit the treetops. As the sun rose higher, beams of light shone down through embracing limbs of the high hemlocks and lit up banks of mountain laurel blossoms stacked along that well-named stream. We caught fish that day, all native brookies, although fly-fishing was a relatively unknown art in Virginia during that era. By sundown the Big Laurel had etched itself into my memory, in the way it only could have in the memory of an impressionable teenager.

I confess that, from the outset, one of my secret objectives in writing about Virginia trout streams was to rediscover the Big Laurel. I looked carefully through every state map, inquired of state fish and game authorities, and interviewed the most knowledgeable old-timers about its location. All I got were blank looks. "Nope. Never heard of it."

At one time I idly considered subtitling my book, "In Search of the Big Laurel," knowing that more pragmatic and professional minds would not allow it. I never did find the Big Laurel. In fact, I'm pretty convinced by this time that it doesn't exist as named, although there's no doubt in my mind that I fished it in 1946. Maybe the name has changed. Maybe the stream was paved over to make way for a rural shopping center. Or maybe it's now just boggy ground overwhelmed by the tailings from some suburban development, although I fervently hope that none of these is the case.

I have recommended various flies for specific streams, mostly because they worked for me on a particular day. But as informed readers know, the most effective fly will depend upon which insects are active on a given stream, the time of year, water temperature, water chemistry, and a number of other subtle variations entomologists are still trying to quantify. I find it beneficial to just sit on a rock a while and study the surface, then to turn over stones for mayfly nymphs, caddis fly cases, and stonefly larvae. If there is no specific hatch, it is my preference to begin fishing with a dry fly such as an Adams or Royal Coachman. Then, when there's no surface activity, trying a variety of nymphs may produce strikes. As the day warms up and duns begin appearing, switch to the dry fly that matches them.

There are some good trout holes beneath this waterfall in the Alleghany Highlands.

Introduction to Virginia Trout Streams

There are various estimates of the amount of trout water in Virginia, perhaps the most realistic being that published by the state's Department of Game and Inland Fisheries. It conservatively lists 2,800 miles of trout water, 500 of it stocked, plus 2,300 miles of wild trout streams. The brilliantly colored little native brook trout is one of Virginia's most precious resources, and as such is carefully nurtured in places like the Shenandoah National Park and on U.S. Forest Service land. That 2,300 miles of wild trout streams is one of the features that makes Virginia trout fishing unusual. Follow just about any stocked stream above the litter line, onto mountainsides steep enough to wrench thigh muscles, and eventually you will come upon near-virgin brook trout fishing.

For those accustomed to the classic streams of Pennsylvania, New England, or Montana, the climate of Virginia often comes as a surprise. You may find yourself fishing in mid-November in short sleeves, with a heavy swarm of olive quills rising from the stream—a delight seldom experienced by northern anglers. Many Virginia stream-lashers prefer the solitude of fall fishing, when they own the stream except for a few bow hunters. There are cold days in autumn, of course, but even then fish become active at midday as the sun's warming effect takes over.

Virginia's low-altitude coastal plain to the east, plus the generally balmy climate, limit trout to the Alleghany and Blue Ridge Mountains in the western part of the state. It is mainly on their high slopes that the water remains cold enough to maintain a year-round trout population. But between these two ranges is the unique limestone belt harboring the spring creeks so productive of healthy browns and rainbows. Virginia's best fishing, theoretically, is from April 1 through mid-June, after which lowland streams have a lower and warmer flow. The resourceful angler can discover excellent fishing at any time of the year, however, by carefully picking high-country streams and keeping a careful eye on the weather, whether in mid-August or mid-December.

The primary objective of this book is to give careful directions for reaching some of Virginia's classic trout streams, including those that lie down unmarked "two-track" dirt roads. Second, the book gives a brief overview of what to expect when you get there. Third, it reflects a glimpse of the intense joy one may derive, not only from the angling, but also from just experiencing the Blue Ridge solitude one finds in Virginia's western mountains.

Management

The hardworking cadre of trout biologists employed by the state work closely with other state agencies and the federal government. They are a dedicated and sensitive group of people, spending increasingly more of their working hours protecting Virginia's fertile aquatic ecosystem against those whose actions would destroy some part of it. Some encroachment upon trout waters is inevitable, however, as Virginia's increasing population puts more pressure on its water resources.

To the credit of the Department of Game and Inland Fisheries, and its helpers in Trout Unlimited, progress is being made. Virginians are waking up to the hard economic fact that trout fishing is an essential part of the state's tourism industry. If the trout environment suffers, the state's economy also suffers. Education of the public is an essential part of the state's program, in addition to following the basics of good trout management.

The three trout-management programs employed in Virginia are put-and-take stocking, protecting wild trout, and put-and-grow stocking. By far the most popular is put-and-take, since newly stocked trout are so easily caught, even by youngsters just beginning the sport. Unfortunately, tradition calls for a dialogue between adult put-'n'-takers that goes something like, "Howdja do?" "Got m' limit," spoken with a knowing tilt of the head. That piece of dialogue has killed more good Virginia trout than disease, high water temperatures, acid rain, and poaching combined. On a stocking day, steely-eyed anglers with chain stringers dragging from their belts patrol the streams wielding spinning rods tipped with steel propeller–driven lures or bait, determined to get their limits. Within a short time the stream is virtually stripped clean of trout. Virginia fly-fishermen avoid these scenes as they would a hog-slaughtering.

Unannounced stocking was recently introduced on the Virginia trout scene. Without a doubt it has helped reduce the crowd waiting on the banks for trout to be dumped from the stocking truck. But there is still the underground network of good ol' boys living near the hatchery who get on the phone to fishing buddies posthaste when they see a hatchery truck pulling out.

A second part of the state's trout-management program is the wild trout project. This encourages the reproducing populations of not only brook but also rainbow and brown trout. Habitats are improved, and regulations protecting developing fish populations are enforced.

These wild trout demand cold, oxygenated water with a clean bottom and good fish cover. The most critical losses of trout in Virginia are caused by raised water temperatures resulting from the naturally warm climate and from drops in water level during the summer. Warming is not so much a problem in the high, shaded mountain streams, which remain below 70 degrees during hot spells. But removing the vegetation along even a short stretch of stream, through logging, farming, or development, can have disastrous results. Temperatures above the low 70s kill trout and encourage rough-fish populations against which trout cannot compete.

Natural siltation, plus more unnatural changes, such as channelization, have cost Virginia many miles of trout streams. Silt cuts down on aquatic-insect populations, an important part of the trout's diet, and also makes reproduction difficult. Trout lay their eggs on gravel bottoms, after which the movement of cold, clean water over the eggs is a necessity. Even a quarter of an inch of silt covering newly hatched eggs can cause 100 percent mortality.

In Virginia today, the deterioration of trout habitats has been reversed, and a steady improvement in water quality is apparent. Another encouraging note: 80 percent of all Virginia wild trout are brook trout, the state's only true native trout. The growth rate of these brookies is phenomenal: 8 to 10 inches by the third year. This fast growth may be due to the longer growing season in Virginia as contrasted to the northern states. In fact, it's safe to say that the Old Dominion offers the best native brook fishing south of New England.

Unfortunately, there has been a tendency toward overfishing of popular wild trout streams. It is critical that wild fish spawn at least once before being creeled, and a 7-inch minimum size limit has helped the wild trout to reach spawning age in such streams. Trout, unlike warm-water fish such as perch and bass, have a very low ability to reproduce.

Perhaps the best solution to sustaining trout populations is encouraging the sportsman's willingness to catch and release. Although this philosophy has caught on in Pennsylvania and New England, very few Virginia anglers return their trout to freedom. When asked about this, a knowledgeable member of the Virginia Tech faculty replied, "I don't believe it's because Virginians are any less enlightened. It's just that no one has told them that catch-and-release is really the ethical way to go." It is interesting to note that Virginia bass fishermen have grasped the advantages of catch-and-release and are beginning to practice it. So there is hope that in the near future, instead of "Caught m' limit," Virginia trout anglers will be proud to say, "Caught and released *twice* my limit."

> **Author's Note** *I once heard an octogenarian in Highland County talk about his experience with trout as a child on the farm. In the evening, after chores were finished, his family would go to the bank of the river, light a fire, and bait up hickory poles. They would then pull in as many brook trout as possible, cleaning them and throwing them into a washtub to be used as a food staple. There may yet be some sentimental holdover of that agrarian attitude, even though there is no longer a rationale for it. Trout farms are now flourishing in western Virginia, producing a high quality of food fish under somewhat more ideal breeding conditions than the fragile ecosystem of the wild.*

On a more upbeat note, Virginia's 2,300 miles of wild trout water are today becoming free of the put-'n'-take mentality. Even some of the deepest backwoods anglers have begun adopting as part of their code the releasing of all the colorful little natives they hook. Hatchery trout are another matter.

One of the pure delights of Virginia fly-fishing is to follow a trail down some hickory ridge and hear the trickle of mountain water in the distance. Approaching closer, you can see the flash of sunlight on falling water. Parting the mountain laurel, you spot the dark shapes of brook trout hovering in some freestone basin, ready to dart away at the slightest movement. Prepare then to spend a day of Appalachian wild trout angling at its finest.

In addition to put-and-take and wild trout projects, there is a third primary management program known as "put-and-grow." This relatively small project involves the stocking of undersized trout that can be fished at a designated time under regulated conditions. Because of the high quality of trout fishing it provides, this program is growing in popularity and scope.

Three somewhat unusual management projects are found on Big Tumbling Creek in the Clinch Mountain Wildlife Management Area, Crooked Creek in Carroll County, and a portion of Wilson Creek in Douthat State Park. These are fee-fishing areas that provide put-and-take fishing on streams stocked several times weekly throughout the season. The fee-fishing season runs from the first Saturday in April through September at Clinch Mounain and Crooked Creek; through October at Douthat. The April opening time is 9 AM. A daily permit is required, in addition to a state fishing license. Because of the encouragement they provide for young anglers and older beginners, two of these streams are included in this book. You can also trek upstream from the fee-fishers and find wild trout when fishing on these streams.

License Requirements

All residents 16 years of age and older are required to possess a state fishing license to fish for trout in Virginia. Persons who fish in designated waters stocked with catchable trout must have a separate trout license. A national forest stamp, available wherever licenses are sold, is required for fishing in most waters within the George Washington and Thomas Jefferson National Forests. Refer to your fishing regulations pamphlet for exemptions.

When fishing in nondesignated trout waters, such as wild trout streams or special-regulations areas, you need only a state fishing license. Many of these special-regulations areas, however, require a signed permit card, obtained from Department of Inland Fisheries offices or from streamside landowners.

Out-of-state anglers fishing stocked waters need to purchase both the nonresident fishing license and the nonresident trout license. The nonresident fishing for wild trout or in special-regulations areas needs only a nonresident fishing license and the appropriate national forest stamps plus special-regulations permits. A money saver (depending on where you plan to fish) is the 5-day license, which substitutes for the yearlong nonresident license for 5 consecutive days. It's good only in unstocked trout waters.

The fee-fishing (pay-as-you-go) areas described require only a state fishing license or a nonresident 5-day license and a daily fishing permit that may be obtained on-site.

Standard Regulations

Virginia's trout season runs all year. The trout-angling time is from 5 AM until one hour after sunset. Minimum size is 7 inches, and creel limit is six per day. All of these standard regulations are subject to change on streams where special regulations, described below, apply.

Special Regulations

In an effort to manage the state's trout waters better and conserve its wild trout population, Virginia has developed a complex system of special regulations. The system is complicated largely because the regulations aim to reflect local conditions and needs. Hence, special regulations, where they apply, vary greatly from region to region and from stream to stream. They include a few catch-and-release areas, special creel limits, length limits designed to protect fish of prime reproductive age, waters where only single-hook artificial lures are permitted, streams with a designated opening day, delayed harvest waters, and pay-as-you-go waters where special day permits are required.

These special regulations and designated waters change fairly frequently, and hence a complete enumeration of them is impossible in this book. Special regulations currently pertaining to waters described are noted in the stream descriptions. However, anglers should consult the booklet *Virginia Freshwater and Saltwater Fishing Regulations,* published by the Virginia

Department of Game and Inland Fisheries, for current and complete information on special regulations. The booklet is given out with fishing licenses and may also be obtained by writing to:

> Virginia Department of Game and Inland Fisheries
> 4010 West Broad Street
> P.O. Box 11104
> Richmond, VA 23230-1104

When special permits are needed for particular streams, they may be obtained by sending your request with a stamped, self-addressed envelope to the appropriate department's field office.

A new regulation specifies that anglers must clean their "keepers" in a special way. In order for trout to be identified and measured, they must not be filleted at streamside and heads and tails are to be left on.

Stream Acidity

During the 1980s there was much talk and media hype about acid rain—to the point that a mention of that phrase was sure to bring a yawn. In Virginia, the response was somewhat more serious, partly because the acid stream damage in the Shenandoah National Park was an acute, high-profile problem. Rain in Virginia has reached a harmful level of acidity, with a pH of 4.27, ten times more acid than normal. In fact, Virginia's Blue Ridge and Western Highlands receive more sulfate pollution than all of the northeastern United States.

Late in the decade, there was an extensive study of stream acidity by the Virginia Department of Game and Inland Fisheries. The Department of Environmental Sciences at the University of Virginia assisted with this study. On April 27, 1987, more than 150 trained Trout Unlimited volunteers began splashing through Virginia streams, tagging trees with numbered station markers, filling coolers with water samples, and writing their observations on prepared data sheets. The samples were turned over to the University of Virginia for evaluation of chemical changes in those streams.

From the 349 streams studied in 1987 under the Virginia Trout Stream Sensitivity Study (VTSSS), 78 were selected by the University of Virginia Department of Environmental Sciences for follow-up analysis, which is still continuing.

VTSSS was the most detailed and inclusive compilation on trout stream acidity ever launched. The initial conclusions were discouraging. Ninety-three percent of the 349 sampled trout streams were sensitive to acidification, while 10 percent were already acidic. If acid deposition continues at 1990 levels into the early decades of the coming century, the future of Virginia's 450 native trout streams looks disastrous. At least 32 percent, and maybe up to 88 percent, of them will become acidic. That is, their ability to neutralize acid fallout will drop to zero.

A recent study found that one-third of all trout streams in Virginia are occasionally or permanently acidic. Most are acidic for only brief periods, such as during heavy runoff. However, 6 percent are permanently acidic, which means they cannot support even the most acid-resistant species, the brook trout.

The study goes on to predict that by the year 2041, the number of permanently acidic streams could rise to 35 percent—that is, if the sulfur deposition that causes acid rain is not reduced. Most sulfates originate from power plants to the west, primarily in Ohio and West Virginia. It will take a 70 percent reduction of sulfur dioxide deposits from 1970 levels just to keep the streams at their present pH. There is a widespread belief that the Clean Air Act has greatly remedied the situation. It has helped, but in spite of such efforts, the acid rain situation remains a serious and growing threat to Virginia's trout streams.

Except on the part of a handful of concerned scientists and Trout Unlimited members, interest in the stream acidity problem has faded. After all, the trout population of an increasingly acidic stream does not die dramatically or suddenly. It dies gradually, fading away from starvation as the aquatic life upon which it feeds disappears. The chart on the next page indicates the pH levels at which specific life-forms die out of acid waters. Of the three trout species prevalent in Virginia, the fragile little native brook trout is, ironically, the last to disappear.

Following release of the crushing volume of data on Virginia's dying trout streams, there was a noisy debate. The media followed this debate for a while and then the picture became somewhat blurred. The general public was left with the comfortable perception that after all, the alarm was no more than the hysteria of a bunch of "environuts." The voices of concerned scientists and informed outdoor sportsmen were muffled.

And then a dramatic incident jolted the public's attention back to the acid stream problem. On March 20, 1993, there was a partial fish kill of recently stocked rainbow trout in some upper Shenandoah Valley streams. Bloated fish were floating in Little Passage Creek, their gills clogged with mucus. Water samples were taken immediately after the kill. They showed average pHs in the low 4s, as opposed to the usual 6 or above. This was attributed to the heavy snows and melting runoff. But these fish were not just slowly dying off, the usual result of acidity. They had been poisoned, and this led to a postmortem to find out what had poisoned them.

The result of examining the killed fish in the lab was unmistakable. These fish had been killed by a toxic level of aluminum. Aluminum? But what about the acid? Aluminum is everywhere, one of the most common

RESILIENCE OF AQUATIC SPECIES TO ACID RAIN

pH	6.5	6.0	5.5	5.0	4.5	4.0	3.5	3.0
Rainbow trout	●	●	○					
Brown trout	●	●	●	○				
Brook trout	●	●	●	●	○			
Smallmouth bass	●	●	○					
Fathead minnow	●	○						
Pumpkinseed sunfish	●	●	●	○				
Yellow perch	●	●	●	●	○			
Bullfrog*	●	●	●	●	○			
Wood frog*	●	●	●	●	●	○		
American toad*	●	●	●	●	○			
Spotted salamander*	●	●	●	○				
Clam**	●	○						
Crayfish**	●	●	○					
Snail*	●	○						
Mayfly	●	●	○					

*Embryonic stage   ● Population intact
**Selected species   ○ Population thinning

elements in the soil. In fact, what we know as clay is mainly hydrated aluminum silicate, considered harmless to life.

But chemists already knew that when aluminum is constantly immersed in acidic water, it is transformed into a number of different molecular forms, some of them highly toxic. At Passage Creek, the inert aluminum clay on the banks had been subjected to runoff water laden with sulfuric and nitric acid solutions. After a while a variant called monomeric aluminum had emerged from the normally harmless soil. Monomeric aluminum is a lethal form of aluminum, perhaps the most lethal of all the active aluminum radicals released that day into Little Passage, Peter's Mill, and also a number of less intensely studied waterways.

Another such example was an insignificant little tributary nearby called Mountain Run. Where aluminum levels turned lethal in this stream, biologists found 62 fish within a mile. Formerly there had been thousands of trout within that mile, which is normal for a stream of that size. Moreover, there were no blacknose dace and no sculpin in Mountain Run.

Aluminum poison kills trout by binding up their gills, causing an unnatural secretion of mucus that eventually suffocates them. If that doesn't finish them, the aluminum compound also causes an imbalance of blood elements, which eventually leads to death.

Adult brook trout can handle such punishment. But let's say the female has just spawned, and there are hundreds of young fry coming out of the gravel redds. They are doomed because of their fragile life stage. There follows a shift in a stream's trout population to older, bigger fish, with brook trout less than two years old out of the picture. Then when insects and other food disappear, you observe two- and three-year-old starving brookies stunted to less than 5 inches. Shortly afterward, you won't catch trout of any size from that stream.

Requiem for the St. Mary's *Flowing down from Blue Ridge Parkway's Fork Mountain Overlook to the Shenandoah Valley floor, the St. Mary's River has the classic look of trout streams in the James River Drainage. But its location in a designated wilderness area did nothing to protect this crystalline stream from acid fallout. The stream is so clear that looking at the water's surface in late-afternoon sunlight, you'll have difficulty seeing where the water leaves off and the air begins. The sad truth, however, is that this perfect clarity is caused by the lack of aquatic life below the surface. The stream is close to being lifeless, with only a rare brook trout clinging to a heroic existence beneath its banks.*

Like many resources of Virginia, the St. Mary's has a history. Once labeled "one of Virginia's higher quality trout streams," it later became known as one of the most acid-sensitive streams in the state. In 1936 a biologist drove his jalopy down a rutted logging trail to the St. Mary's River and took a count of mayflies per square foot. He recorded a healthy 6.95 Ephemerella, *many more than enough for maintenance of the vigorous brook trout population there at that time. In 1977 the last mayfly was sighted along the stream.*

Returning to the St. Mary's after two years, I had the feeling of someone looking for his old homeplace and finding it gone. No amount of skillful maneuvering of my Woolly Bugger produced the reassuring flash of scarlet and silver of even one hungry brook trout. It was difficult to reconcile the quiet beauty of this St. Mary's Wilderness Area and its river with the steady rain of sulfate and nitrate particles still falling there today. With regret I have eliminated it from this book as a fishable stream.

RESURRECTION OR REPRIEVE?

I wrote the previous description after a discouraging trip to the St. Mary's in 1993. The situation is essentially the same, but now there's a flicker of hope for this matriarch of Virginia brook trout streams.

Highland County has more than its share of outstanding trout streams.

On March 20, 1999, headwaters and tributaries of the St. Mary's were bombarded with 140 tons of ground limestone, dropped by a helicopter carrying a 2-ton bucket. As the dark clouds of crusher run fell from the sky, some equally murky questions arose about the St. Mary's. How long will it take for this acid rain–abused stream to come back to near neutral? Two days after the drop, the lower St. Mary's registered a robust 6.37 pH. National forest fisheries biologists believe there may be an explosion of brook trout during the next spawning cycle. The catchable population will probably mature in two years.

How long will the treatment last? The effects of such liming projects have lasted from five to eight years depending upon the intensity of acid particulate being dumped on it. But the cost was $90,000, and so there's no thought of continuing the drops. The deposit had to be from the air, as the St. Mary's flows through a wilderness area with no vehicles allowed. Other acid-abused streams would not require such elaborate measures.

A study conducted recently by the University of Virginia produced some chilling statistics. By 2041, 22 percent of Virginia's 304 trout streams would be acid dead. And even now 6 percent of them are chronically acidic. Rick Webb, a coauthor of the study, said the western slope streams along the Blue Ridge are the most susceptible to acid precipitation because the quartzite and sandstone bedrock common here is incapable of neutralizing the acid.

One longtime resident here began guiding fly-fishers in the Blue Ridge

Mountains when he retired from farming 23 years ago. The St. Mary's was once his favorite destination, but now he never fishes it. The rainbow trout disappeared during the mid-1980s, then the brown trout. Now only the hardy little native brookies remain, as they are more resistant to acid. On my last trip I hooked a couple of these tough little survivors, but their disproportionately large heads were a sign of malnutrition. I vowed not to disturb them again for a few more years.

The St. Mary's was an ideal choice for what is essentially an experiment in resurrecting acid-abused streams. Its streambed is hard, insoluble quartzite, with no buffering property. It's a relatively large stream, as Virginia brook trout streams go. It flows through a wilderness area of singular beauty. And it was once a premier native trout fishery.

On the downside, such liming treatments are only a temporary answer. As one official put it, "We're just trying to hold the pieces together until something can be done about the larger issue." The larger issue, of course, is the outpouring of nitrates and sulfates from coal-burning power plants plus other sources. The answer to such acidification is not clear. It may lie in new technology, which will clean up pollution at the smokestacks and exhausts at less cost to owners. The bottom line is the necessity of reducing acid-producing emissions through recycling, clean air legislation, an informed public, plus whatever other means become available.

The Death of Roaring Fork *In May 1994 I revisited one of the most beautiful rhododendron waterways in western Virginia. Called Roaring Fork, it flows through a wilderness area within the Jefferson National Forest. With me were two members of the Galax Trout Unlimited chapter.*

As usual, we were dazzled by the emerald and white flow of this little stream. But the more we fished, the farther our hearts sank into our hip boots. The greenish white tint was due somewhat to the strands of algae trailing from the boulders, one symptom of acidification.

There were no minnows present, and the only insect life was one frazzled little yellow stonefly. In one impressive pool beneath a rock bluff, a group of dwarf brook trout were thrusting their heads out of the water. I caught one, and handling it very carefully, found it to have spawning colors, indicating it to be at least a year old. But it was only 5 inches long.

I later asked a state freshwater biologist about the Roaring Fork brookies' peculiar habit of sticking their heads out of the water. He said, "They do this when there is no available food beneath the surface, and they need to look for terrestrial insects."

After this trip to Roaring Fork I eliminated the stream from my book as a fishable stream.

The aluminum hit on Shenandoah Valley streams carries a strong message. In less than a decade since the VTSSS study, streams that had normal trout populations are lifeless. Not only trout, but other species of fish have vanished. This in spite of no logging upstream, no building of roads, and no other form of pollution. The conclusion reached by freshwater biologists is clear: acid runoff producing toxic levels of aluminum is an increasingly common phenomenon.

When asked about the eventual effect upon the water table, one such biologist shrugged his shoulders and said, "We don't know." A government administrator was somewhat more specific about the future. His answer was the question, "Is it possible that the brook trout is about to become an endangered species?"

The fish kill at Passage Creek was disputed by the usual critics crying for "more complete data before we can reach any conclusion." On one occasion a minor misquote in the media was singled out for scorching criticism, obscuring the real message of the article. The usual cycle of debate and apathy has again pushed the Passage Creek horror to the bottom of the public's list of priorities. And at this writing the matter rests there until another fish kill, or worse, brings it back into the media spotlight.

The answer? It has been obvious for some time: Reduce the levels of nitrogen oxide and sulfur dioxide being released into the atmosphere by burning fossil fuel, on both a local and national level. We can agree that further studies of acid rain are needed. But in the meantime, inertia is killing off one of Virginia's most valuable and colorful forms of wildlife.

I asked a University of Virginia environmental scientist, "Doesn't anyone care?" His answer was, "Sure. A lot of people do care. But they're forced to balance nature's gain against commerce's loss. And sometimes nature loses out."

Hatches

The term *hatch* normally refers to duns or immature adults of aquatic insects reaching the surface. The four species of flies most noteworthy to Virginia anglers are mayflies, stoneflies, caddis flies, and the amorphous group called midges. Significant hatches may be observed along the Blue Ridge 7 or 8 months out of the year, whenever the water temperature is above 50 degrees. A groggy olive quill has even been observed during Christmas week, looking as though it regretted the decision to emerge.

Nymphs are present beneath the surface virtually every day of the year, and thus a skillful wet-fly fisherman will naturally outperform the dry-fly angler when their successes are averaged over a season. But when an active hatch is on the water, the dry fly is king. It's hard to beat the surface pop-and-splash drama of a day when spinners are swarming above the water, a spinner being a mating adult male, distinguished by its glassy clear wings. The so-called spinner fall refers mainly to the adult females falling exhausted with outstretched wings onto the surface to deposit their eggs. One Virginia veteran observer of spinner falls remarked, "If a trout won't take my dry fly, he's not worth catching anyhow." The prudent course may be to take along a mix of common wet and dry patterns, predominantly mayflies, to avoid being skunked on a given day.

The mayfly table below does not include every species found in Virginia. Rather, these are the species capably observed by Stephen W. Hiner, a member of the entomology department at Virginia Tech and an avid stream-lasher. He describes his listing as the mayfly "biggies" for fly-fishers matching the hatches in Virginia's trout streams.

The pale evening or sulphur dun is one of the more significant Virginia mayflies. It is found on all stream types and plays a key role in the Shenandoah National Park stream ecosystem. It is a generally exciting and dependable hatch in the Appalachians.

Mayflies (Ephemeroptera)

Scientific Name	Common Name	Emergence	Location
Epeorus pleuralis	quill gordon	April	HF, MF
Paraleptophlebia spp.	blue quill	April	HF, MF
Epeorus vitreus	gray-winged yellow quill	May	HF, MF
Stenonema vicarium	march brown	May	HF, MF
Ephemerella dorothea	pale evening dun (sulfur)	May	all
Ephemerella berneri	Smith River hendrickson	May	Smith River
Ephemerella guttulata	green drake	May	all
Ephemerella rotunda	light hendrickson	May–June	L, T
Stenacron spp.	light cahill	June	HF, MF
Isonychia spp.	mahogany dun	June–Sept.	MF, LF
Trichorythodes spp.	Trico	Aug.–Sept.	L
Baetis complex	olive quill	anytime	all
Drunella spp.	blue-winged olive	uncertain	T
Callibaetis spp.	speckled quill	summer–fall	ponds

HF: headwater freestone streams; **MF:** midreach freestone streams; **T:** tailwaters; **L:** alkaline, limestone waters; **spp.:** reference is to various species within the genus named

The green drake, prolific in more northern latitudes, isn't a big hatch in Virginia, though some anglers consider it essential on the Whitetop Laurel.

Mahogany duns are probably more important in the nymph than the dun stage. The nymphs crawl out of the water onto stones and bridge supports, making the dun less available to fish. The Lead-Winged Coachman best approximates it.

The speckled quill occurs in every "trout pond" in Virginia, sometimes in great numbers. It's usually most active in late summer and fall.

Below the Gathright Dam on the Jackson River, at least two species of blue-winged olives occur in staggering numbers. They are probably one reason this stretch of water is becoming one the state's most successful stock-and-grow projects.

Much of the mayfly activity in Virginia is still under active study, and more about it will be known as fly-fishing gains in popularity here. Virginia, however, will probably never have the great volume of insect lore that's been recorded in such states as Pennsylvania. There is no counterpart here to Charlie Meck's sharp-eyed cadre of Pennsylvania bug-watchers armed with notebook and pencil. There are, nonetheless, some highly authoritative academic entomologists who have added to the literature and corrected some taxonomic errors in the mayfly arena, in particular Reese Voshell, professor of entomology and aquatic-insect study at Virginia Tech, and Boris Kondratieff, who is now at Colorado State. Kondratieff was one of Voshell's first graduate students at Tech during the early '80s, when they worked together on an extensive study of aquatic insects along the Blue Ridge watersheds.

STONEFLIES (PLECOPTERA)
There have been 149 species of stoneflies reported in Virginia, the highest number from any state. By contrast, 77 species have been reported in Kentucky, 130 in North Carolina, and 106 in West Virginia. The wealth of stoneflies in Virginia is due to the variety of topography found here—including six major types, ranging from Coastal Plain to Piedmont Plateau through Blue Ridge, Ridge, and Valley, and, most importantly, Appalachian Plateau.

Add to that eight major river basins, including the New River, second-oldest river on earth next to the Nile. These watersheds drain from a height of 5,729 feet atop Mount Rogers, down to the Coastal Plain's sea level. There are 80 species of stoneflies in the central Appalachians and Piedmont Plateau foothills alone. It's no wonder biologists rank this area one of the richest in North America in terms of different plant and animal species.

Virginia native trout had enjoyed a stonefly feast for millennia before the arrival of Sir Walter Raleigh. Despite this bonanza of stonefly species, however, there are really only four basic stonefly patterns Virginia fly-fishers need to concentrate on:

- **Winter and spring stoneflies,** which continue to emerge through December. Just before the Christmas holidays, Smith River browns have been observed feeding on the adults.
- **Giant stoneflies** are found in most headwater streams. During their nymph stage they are best imitated with the Black Stone nymph, a real gulp for brookies.
- **Common stoneflies** live up to their name in both small and medium-sized Virginia freestone streams. They are the most colorful of the stoneflies, occurring in mottled patterns of black, brown, and yellow. Many of the more popular realistic patterns are tied to imitate common stoneflies.
- **Little yellow stoneflies,** a branch of the Perlodidae family, become most significant as adults in freestone headwater streams from May through July.

CADDIS FLIES (TRICHOPTERA)

The two streams in Virginia with the best caddis fly potential are the Smith and the Jackson, the former having the most prolific hatches, and the Jackson providing the greater variety.

The net-spinner caddis flies include the spotted sedge and little sister sedge. These occur in most waters and emerge from April through July. Among the tube case makers, there are a couple of caddis fly genera worth mentioning. One is the autumn mottled sedge. It emerges around September and October. The plain brown sedge and American grannom are a couple of other spring-emerging caddis flies of localized importance in certain freestone streams.

MIDGES

Although the label *midge* is commonly applied to the small slappable insects frequenting streams and the anatomies of trout anglers, there is only one true midge family, the Chironomidae. Blackflies and crane flies are often mistakenly called midges, along with some of the tinier species of mayflies, and there are many midges that defy any systematic labeling.

These gnatty species are common to Virginia streams and add much to the pleasure of all Virginia anglers—including that peculiar breed who crunches through fringes of January ice. Midges are all quite small and require a special kind of fishing tactic that Stephen Hiner labels "insane behavior," referring to the reduction of everything to its smallest common denominator: light line, 7X tippet, number 20 or number 22 flies. Even if you have excellent vision, you'll find some craziness involved in midge fishing, because getting close enough to see such a tiny fly means standing very close indeed to the fish.

TERRESTRIALS

During certain times of the year every Virginia trout stream is dependent upon terrestrials—either partially or completely—for fish forage. Certain streams on certain late-summer days must be fished exclusively with terrestrials. Mossy Creek during hopper time is an outstanding example.

One unique feeding pattern observed involves trout under dense overhangs taking only specific terrestrials, such as beetles or ants, while their brethren in midstream are feeding on aquatic insects. Several—but not all—of the key Virginia terrestrials are: hoppers, crickets, leafhoppers, beetles, moths, inchworms, and ants.

Suppose none of the above insect patterns seems to be moving on a stream? One good way to test trout activity is with an Adams number 18, fished as an attractor. If the feeding action on a particular day is wet all the way, a Muddler Minnow number 16 or 18 worked with a vibration from the wrist is sometimes an accurate test of the day's angling potential.

Safety

COLD-WEATHER HAZARDS

Slipping and taking a dunking in electrifyingly cold trout water is one of the minor discomforts of summertime angling. On an October day when the temperature is around 45 degrees, it becomes a matter of somewhat more than discomfort. Many anglers do not realize that hypothermia can result from air temperatures in the 40s. After thrashing out of an icy plunge pool in autumn or winter, you can have more than just chattering teeth. After the onset of severe shivering, a dunking victim may have difficulty walking and speaking. Next come drowsiness and progressive confusion, sometimes even leading to hallucination. In severe cases there may be cardiac arrest.

For mild hypothermia, with a body temperature down in the 90–95 degree range, the condition may not seem serious. The victim is conscious, fairly alert, and shivering. A little exercise, walking briskly and flailing the arms, should help start the blood flowing. But even a mild drop in temperature can lead to some disorientation. That increasing feeling of confusion makes finding your way out of some remote native trout stream with little or no trail a more serious matter. With a breeze blowing and a drop in temperature as shadows lengthen, soaking-wet clothing becomes a critical health problem.

Prevention is always best, and wearing felt soles on your waders can often prevent a bone-jarring wet back flip. In cool weather wear insulated waders or thermal underwear, or both. A wading staff does not have to be an elaborate and costly piece of hardware. A hickory stick with a hole drilled in the head to accommodate a loop of thong, plus a rubber cane tip, will work fine. Wading across the current in a spring freshet often requires that tripodal support from a good staff firmly placed downstream. With a thong sufficient to fit over the head, it can be slung out of the way until needed by even the most macho image-conscious stream-lasher.

Despite all precautions, you're going to fall in. There's never any doubt it will happen—usually when you have just placed your boot on what appears to be the most secure and dry stone in the stream. Whoops! Now you're in up to your armpits, and it's Virginia Appalachian spring cold. What now? After you've crawled out on the bank, it's time to take from your fishing vest that medicine vial of strike-anywhere matches dipped in paraffin. (It helps that the vial top was also sealed with melted paraffin.) Or you may prefer a small butane lighter, sealed in a Ziploc bag with some bottle-cap candles.

Whatever the method, start a fire, fast, with the usual precautions of a stone ring surrounded by bare ground. Putting modesty aside, wring out at least some of the wet clothing and hang it by the fire. When your teeth have stopped playing "Night on Bald Mountain" and your clothes are damp but warm enough to put back on, head back to your vehicle. There you will find that complete change of dry clothing you always carry, even in July. (You do, don't you? Anyone who's really needed a dry set of clothing, including underdrawers, is never again without them.) Alcoholic beverages are out following a soaking, as they lower body temperature. On the other hand, a thermos of hot coffee on the tailgate will help with both morale and physical discomfort.

Most household fever thermometers don't register below 94 degrees and may hide a case of even mild hypothermia. When hypothermia progresses without treatment, confusion gives way to unconsciousness accompanied by shock. It's then a life-or-death situation. If you encounter someone obviously suffering from prolonged exposure, he or she should be immediately transported to the nearest medical facility with as little jostling as possible. Severe hypothermia is a tricky matter, and the difficult treatment should be attempted by a layperson only if no medical help is available. It calls for warmth in any form, including blankets, a car heater, a sleeping bag, and even body-to-body transfer of heat.

In Virginia's western mountains, you may be well over an hour's walk from your vehicle, whether in a federal park preserve or a national forest primitive area. In fact, that's where you'll find the best native brook trout fishing. Before leaving the pavement, always notify someone where you will be and when. Shenandoah National Park rangers urge you to inform them before hiking in to one of their streams alone—which makes good sense. Crawling 4 miles with hypothermia or a fractured leg is much less desirable than just waiting for help to come when you don't show up back at your vehicle.

POISONOUS SNAKES

The southern Appalachians are home to only two species of poisonous snakes, the timber rattler and the copperhead. Although it is not as irritable or venomous as its western diamondback cousin, the timber rattler's bite is much more serious than that of the copperhead. There is no recent history of anyone's dying from the bite of a copperhead in Virginia. Rattlers are much less commonly encountered than copperheads, though state Inland Fisheries field-workers don't agree that holds true in trout-stream terrain. Both of these venomous species are slow-moving and anxious to get out of your way.

Check with local landowners or park personnel to see if there has been a problem with venomous snakes on the stream you're planning to fish. If so, either change your plans or be extra cautious where you step. In snake country, the wading staff doubles as a probe for poking vigorously into high grass or rock piles before taking a blind step. A good staff will also serve as a warning when rapped smartly on the stones or thrashed against the weeds. Most of the time snakes will depart when given such a warning. An exception is a snake caught out of its den by a cool snap, when it will be sluggish and less likely to move away. That may be a good time to stay in midstream.

There are 30 species of snakes in Virginia, many of which are often mistaken for copperheads. One of the startling copperhead look-alikes on trout streams are northern water snakes, which proliferate there. These are non-venomous but highly destructive to trout, particularly at low water. If the water snakes are actively feeding, you may as well leave the stream.

There's so much medical controversy surrounding the use of tourniquets, cut-and-suck snakebite kits, ice packs, and other treatment methods that it's hard to distinguish which, if any, is the preferred treatment. Few physicians disagree, however, with immobilizing the bite victim and carrying him or her to a medical facility equipped with antivenin as rapidly as possible.

TICKS

As if Rocky Mountain spotted fever weren't enough, a new tick hazard, Lyme disease, has invaded the woods. Both ailments may be contracted in Virginia's forests. Lyme disease has increased here at an alarming rate. In one small mountain community, four cases were reported within one month.

Luckily, scientists have accumulated a great deal of knowledge about this disease since it was first discovered in Lyme, Connecticut, in 1976. Caused by a tick-borne spirochete bacterium, *Borrelia burgdorferi,* like any bacterial disease it can be cured by antibiotics, preferably high doses in the early stages. The two ticks most likely to carry Lyme disease in Virginia are the *Ixodes dammini* and the more prevalent *Ixodes scapulari* (deer tick), both tiny enough to be comfortable on the head of a pin.

Because the carriers are smaller than any ticks we are accustomed to, it is best to wear light-colored clothing on which they may be spotted more easily. Wear long-sleeved shirts, preferably tight around the wrists. Insect repellent works on these small bloodsuckers, especially DEET in concentrations of 30 percent or more.

Most active in Virginia in May through October, ticks may also be found here up through late fall because of the warm winters. It's a good idea for you and your fishing partner to check one another's clothes frequently. When you get home strip down and put your clothes into the washer as soon as possible. Check yourself over for tiny crawlers, and then scrub down thoroughly in the shower.

If in spite of these precautions you find a tick biting you, gently remove it by pulling upward with tweezers or facial tissue. Take care not to break it off, and don't bother with matches, Vaseline, or some of the other jackleg methods formerly recommended. Save the tick in a jar of alcohol in case you begin showing any of the Lyme disease symptoms.

During the first stage of the illness there is the classic rash, which expands slowly and fades in the center, giving it a bull's-eye appearance. You may also get flulike first-stage symptoms: slight fever, stiff muscles, fatigue, headaches, and swollen lymph nodes. It may take several days to weeks for these to appear, and then take care. The symptoms vanish, lulling you into thinking there's no problem. Treatment is much more effective during this first stage, so don't ignore the symptoms. Second-stage symptoms appear weeks or even months later. Now you may have headaches, stiff neck, sleeplessness, and lack of coordination. Watch for dizziness, weakness, and irregular heartbeat, all and any of which may disappear and reappear without warning. The third stage appears as chronic arthritis, especially of the knees, shoulders, and wrists. There may be serious neurological problems as well. The invasion of Lyme disease into internal organs such as the brain or heart may be fatal unless treated with massive doses of intravenous penicillin. Even when confined to the joints, the bacteria may cause an immune response resulting in permanent crippling polyarthritis.

More prevalent than Lyme disease, but less talked about, is Rocky Mountain spotted fever, carried by the larger wood tick. Symptoms are fever, rash, generalized aches and pains, and headache. See a physician if any of these occurs after a tick bite.

Be aware of Lyme disease and Rocky Mountain spotted fever, but don't listen to the hysteria that surrounds them, and know enough about the diseases to take precautions against catching them. Then go out and enjoy the hopper season along Virginia's trout streams, including the ones with brushy banks.

Equipment

FLY-RODS

A good average rod on Virginia streams would be a 7 1/2-foot 5-weight. Some highly successful Old Dominion stream-lashers use a 9-foot 4-weight, others a 6 1/2-foot 3-weight. The longer rod keeps your line higher, and that's an advantage when fishing nymphs up off the bottom. Also you get a longer cast on rivers such as the Jackson and the Smith. The short rod keeps you out of the hemlock limbs and gives you a quick little roll cast, which avoids hooking your fly in the ever-present bushes along the little native trout headwaters. I prefer to use two rods, an 8 1/2-foot 4- to 5-weight and a 6-foot 3-weight, each of which has its place.

The introduction of graphite rods by Fenwick in 1973 produced a revolution in rod making even more significant than the first use of fiberglass 25 years before. By weight, graphite is two-and-a-half times stronger than fiberglass and four times stronger than steel. And still graphite affords a 25 percent saving in weight over fiberglass.

Is the graphite rod, as some maintain, the best fishing instrument ever devised? Many bamboo purists will go to the mat with you on that. But it is a fact that graphite is more responsive than either cane or fiberglass. Testing has shown that it suffers less from material fatigue than bamboo or fiberglass. One study showed that fiberglass will soften with use and age by about 8 percent, bamboo will soften about 6 percent, and graphite less than 1 percent. Thus, a graphite rod will retain its original action longer than any of the others. Graphite fibers, which are incorporated into the rod blanks, are extremely thin—about 0.0003 inch. For the construction of the blank, the fibers are arranged along the axis of the blank and impregnated with epoxy resin. It is this lamination of many tiny fibers that gives graphite rods their great strength.

Many experts report that graphite makes it easier for them to cast in tight loops, which translates to greater accuracy. They also say that the graphite damps out better at the end of a cast, cutting down the tip vibration that often shortens distance. Fiberglass was always notorious for this vibrating effect, producing ripples in the line.

The experts aside, fiberglass should not be sold short. For a beginning fly-fisher, it is perfectly adequate, and even an experienced fly-caster's reliable old glassie may tenaciously hold its place beside his graphite and cane models. For one with only a casual interest in the sport, the price of a glass rod is certainly attractive, often only half that of a comparable graphite rod. A new generation of glass rods, although expensive, rivals the performance of graphite and has a generally softer action. One manufacturer is Lamiglas in Woodland, WA, who may be contacted at jposey@lamigles.com.

Stephen Hiner, entomologist at Virginia Polytechnic Institute, releases a native brookie caught on a December morning.

Most graphite rods are gray, the natural color of the material, with a clear finish. However, there are more color variations reaching the market. The better blanks have color impregnated throughout the material, while less expensive brands coat the color on the outside.

The 1990s have seen rapid advances in graphite manufacturing, with lighter, stronger, yet thinner rods—a spin-off from defense and space research. Stronger and lighter-weight graphite fiber developed for use in Stealth bombers and space capsules has made these higher-quality graphite rods possible. Because of their lightweight material, these newer rods are extremely sensitive.

Should you buy a fast- or slow-action rod? The *action* of a rod refers to the motion of the portion that actually flexes. With a fast rod, only a part of the tip section flexes appreciably. This gives you a tighter loop and faster action. It may actually increase your casting distance, but it means you must be more tightly in command of your casting action. On the debit side, a fast rod tends to cause the line to shoot out and hit the surface, making a delicate presentation a little trickier.

A slower rod is more forgiving and allows you somewhat more leeway in your motion. There's also less possibility of the wind knots experienced with a tighter loop, but most experts agree that the faster rod is generally more accurate, although they will admit that accuracy depends upon the user. Slower-action rods produce bigger loops, which have more wind resistance, and even without the wind tend to wander a little more. On the positive side, a slower rod, with its bigger loop, allows you to make a more delicate presentation, with the fly drifting down to the surface in a more lifelike manner.

What this debate all comes down to is that when buying a high-quality rod, particularly a custom-made one, you should always try a number of similar models. Select the type that best matches your casting technique and feels right to you.

Choosing the right graphite rod is a highly subjective exercise. It comes down to your personal preference, plus what your pocketbook can bear. Many average-to-good fly-casters are content with a $70 department store rod, despite giving up quality of the reel seat, line guides, and the graphite blank itself. Such a rod is good for beginners but does not produce the best action and is not really durable.

A fly-rod from a custom maker will probably not cost less than $200, with dollars added for embellishments such as better blanks, silicon carbide line guides, and cork and wood reel seats. But with proper care, such a rod will last the rest of your life and may be passed down to the next generation in pretty good shape.

LINE, LEADERS, AND REELS

Perhaps the most confusing choice for the fly-fisher is line. From a dazzling array of weights, colors, tapers, and synthetic materials, you are expected to choose just the right one. As a rule of thumb, the rod, plus the size of flies you favor, will narrow down the choice. Be prepared to downsize to number 20 flies on days when the fish spurn your larger offerings. Fly lines run from number 1 to 14, with the smaller numbers denoting lighter and finer lines. Size 4 or smaller will drop even a tiny number 20 Adams on the water in a gentle and lifelike manner. Size 6 line has enough heft to carry larger streamers and hoppers on big brown trout waters and will also get by handling smaller flies adequately when necessary.

The choice of floating or sinking line may be dictated by where the trout are feeding on a particular day. Because it feels slightly heavier on the rod than the floating variety, a sinking line may be a few grains lighter than the corresponding number of floating line. One answer to the float-versus-sink choice is to load two reels, one with each type, and switch reels on the stream as dictated by where the trout are feeding that day.

Line taper is another consideration. Some beginners start with an untapered, or level, line, which will work fine. Later, when they have more feeling for the finer points, a double-taper is a good choice; that is, a line tapered at both ends. It's the most economical because when one end starts to wear, you can just swap to the other end, doubling the life of your line. The belly, or middle section, seldom shows any appreciable wear.

What about color? You have a choice of lines ranging from mahogany through blue, green, yellow, orange, or white. You also have your choice of many highly vocal opinions on line color. Some anglers swear by floating green, claiming it blends in with the overhead vegetation. Others claim that white will scare fish away. Maybe so, but a white line is always visible to you, and adding on the length of the leader, you can calculate just where even the tiniest fly is located on the water if you can see your line. A compromise here is an off-white or light tan line, which still offers visibility without calling attention to itself. These lighter colors are used by some experienced trout guides in Virginia, with consistent success.

Some lightweight-line users favor the weight-forward over the double-taper line, claiming it gives them a longer cast faster and works well into the wind. For the small Virginia streams, however, a double-taper works fine, with the small difference in weight-forward not really mattering on a number 4 through 6 line. And in some cases the line debate becomes academic, since short casting room requires a dependence upon the 8 or 10 feet of monofilament leader.

On a given day, the length and weight of your leader may have the greatest influence upon success and failure. For small dry flies, a knotless taper starting from a 0.02-inch butt and going down to at least 5X is best. For some of the more fickle feeders, a 6X is favored by some anglers, even with the frail tippet's tendency to curl. When you are fishing a sinking line, attaching a fluorescent marker to your leader will improve chances of detecting a subtle underwater tug.

Fly reels are sometimes taken for granted, looked upon as spools for storing line. However, with reels, as elsewhere, there are always better and worse. Some cheaper models allow the line to jam up between the spool and sides. If you've just hooked that citation brown that's eluded you all season, and he's headed for underwater brush, a jammed reel means goodbye. Also take a look at the starting drag, since that same big brown will break the leader without a light starting drag.

OTHER EQUIPMENT

Hip boots are adequate for wading on most Virginia mountain streams, and there may be August days when it's a relief to step out into midstream shod only in shorts and felt-soled wading shoes. On some of the larger streams, such as the Jackson and the Smith, chest waders are necessary. On a frosty day, chest waders can be a boon if you slip and fall into even a small stream. Yes, Virginia, there is some of the world's slipperiest algae on your rocks, even during cold weather. A dry backside sometimes makes carrying the extra weight of insulated chest waders worthwhile. Speaking of which, felt soles are well worth whatever they may cost, in terms of fewer bruises or broken bones.

One very essential piece of gear is a set of surgical forceps, dangling from your fishing vest. For removing a hook quickly without harming the trout, these are indispensable. Many expert anglers nowadays use their forceps so deftly that they never have to touch the fish and have given up landing nets in favor of an accurate grab of the hook with their forceps while the trout is still waterborne.

Fishing vests, front- or rear-loaded fly carriers, and fishing hats are a matter of personal choice, with unlimited variety. It may be wise to remember, however, that Virginia landowners are mostly mountain-grown farmers. To approach them asking permission to fish while wearing a getup worthy of Stewart Granger, the Great White Angler, may not be the wisest way to go.

In choosing fly-fishing equipment, one rule to keep in mind is that there are few rules. The cookbook approach is simply not appropriate, and it's best to experiment with rods, lines, leaders, and all the other paraphernalia of trout angling until you're comfortable with what you have.

Maps and Highway Directions

This book contains maps of each of the six regions covered, plus individual maps of some of the most important streams. Often, however, you will find it useful to refer to more detailed topographic maps.

Traditionally the topographic maps published by the United States Geological Survey (USGS) have been the most useful sources of information for anglers. The USGS has published several series, but the most common series today in Virginia is the 7½-minute series, with a scale of 1 inch per 2,000 feet. These maps can tell a great deal about a stream—whether it flows through open or forested terrain, how steeply it drops, where tributaries enter. They can also help you find the easiest access to streams by showing roads, trails, and power-line cuts. USGS maps do, however, have their drawbacks—notably in the fact that they are sometimes out of date and do not show some current trails and landmarks. Nevertheless, they remain important tools for anglers, and the appropriate 7½-minute series USGS quadrangle is listed at the beginning of each stream description.

Individual USGS maps are available at some bookstores and sporting goods stores and can also be ordered from:

Distribution Branch
United States Geological Survey
Box 25286
Federal Center
Denver, CO 80225
303-236-7477

This office will also provide, free of charge, an index and catalog of USGS maps of Virginia.

The best and most convenient collection of topographic maps in one volume is the *Virginia Atlas and Gazetteer*. It is available in most sporting goods stores for $16.95 or may be ordered from:

The DeLorme Mapping Company
P.O. Box 298
Yarmouth, ME 04096
207-846-7000

DeLorme map references are also given for each stream described.

Ordinary road maps, published by the state of Virginia, oil companies, or automobile clubs, can also help provide stream access information. The Virginia Department of Transportation, 1401 East Broad Street, Richmond, VA 23219, publishes inexpensive county road maps that can be quite useful to anglers.

Throughout the text, highways and roads are indicated by the following letter symbols:

I   Interstate
US   US Highway
VA   State Highway
VA(s) Secondary State Highway
FR   National Forest Road

2 | Shenandoah National Park Area

The 200,000 acres of hardwood forest within the park boundaries includes one of the few sizable areas of wild trout habitat in the eastern United States. Since it's located only a short distance from Washington, D.C., Baltimore, and other large metropolitan areas, the park and its environs play host to millions of visitors each year. In spite of this pressure, the native brook trout population is thriving, due to careful management and cooperation from the angling public. There are more than 90 streams within the total brook trout ecosystem, all of which are managed and now open year-round. Harvest is allowed on the larger streams. Several streams, such as the Rapidan, are designated catch-and-release, but the concept of carefully handling and releasing fish is fostered within the entire fishery. Park regulations are the same as those of the Virginia Department of Game and Inland Fisheries.

These picturesque freestone mountain streams do not contain an abundance of food, particularly when compared to Virginia's rich limestone-spring waters. The lack of natural foods keeps the trout in the Shenandoah Park constantly on the move in search of the best feeding station, with the largest fish occupying the most rewarding spots. This constant rotation of hungry fish makes for some exciting action and furnishes enough nourishment to keep the brookies thriving and growing.

For the most part these are hike-in fishing locations, requiring a little foresight in putting together equipment that is easily packed down fairly steep trails—and, what is even more important, back up again.

The two visitor information centers within the park offer maps and advice on current fishing conditions on specific streams. Since certain fisheries are closed during low water, it is always a good idea to check before hiking in. Another source of fishing data on the park is the book *Trout Fishing in the Shenandoah National Park*, by Harry Murray (Edinburg, Virginia: Shenandoah Publishing Company, 1989). This publication gives detailed directions on which trails to follow from the Skyline Drive down to 28 streams, as well as how to reach them from the lower park boundary.

The following section covers six of the best Shenandoah Park waters, plus nearby Smith Creek, presenting a cross section of stream types from the robust Whiteoak Canyon Run to the reclusive East Hawksbill Creek. The southernmost portion of the park is within the James River Drainage, and two of the best streams in that area (Meadow Run and the North Fork of the Moorman's River) are described in chapter 4.

BIG RUN

Stream Type Freestone

Maps USGS Mcgaeysville; DeLorme 67

Access At this writing, there is no access from downstream, as park property is bounded by rigidly posted private land. This portion of the stream is known to virtually dry up in summer, and therefore has no carryover of trout. Even though there may be access at some time in the future, with change of land ownership, the fishing doesn't begin until around 3 miles upstream.

From the Big Run overlook on the Skyline Drive, just south of milepost 81, take the Big Run Loop Trail 2.2 miles, to where it runs into the Big Run Portal Trail. Stay on this until the trail veers away from the stream, then follow the stream's bank on downstream. Allow yourself enough time and energy for the muscle-wrenching climb back up to the overlook. It is not a wise idea to be caught in here after dark: The timber rattler is a protected species in the park.

Fishing Big Run is an adventure, taking you into a relatively untouched section of the Shenandoah Park if you persevere downstream past Rocky Mountain and Lewis Peak. It is encouraging to see a stream bank this close to the eastern megalopolis without a sign of a footpath or other human usage. Follow the stream down from the Skyline Drive as far as you think will allow you a good day's fishing back upstream. At first Big Run may be disappointingly small along the Big Run Portal Trail, and it's necessary to go at least as far down as Rocky Mountain Run to begin serious fishing.

You will encounter steep going, with a series of rapids and plunge pools. The surroundings are rugged. On the north bank will be a jagged bluff with a 10-foot-high stone Indian's profile. It is recommended that you go past that. Doing so will necessitate climbing up some 20-foot boulders and sliding down the other side, but it's preferable to traveling the precipitous bank above. A strong wading staff is a valuable piece of equipment on this stretch, both in the water and on dry land.

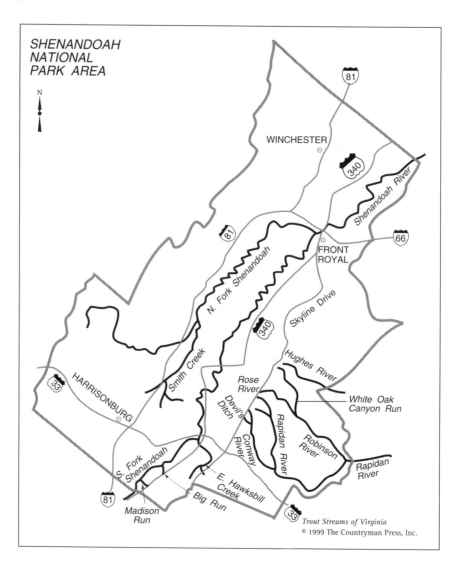

SHENANDOAH
NATIONAL
PARK AREA

N

WINCHESTER

81

340

Shenandoah River

81

N. Fork Shenandoah

FRONT
ROYAL

66

Skyline Drive

340

Hughes River

Smith Creek

HARRISONBURG

33

Rose
River

White Oak
Canyon Run

Devil's
Ditch

Conway
River

Rapidan River

Robinson
River

S. Fork
Shenandoah

E. Hawksbill
Creek

Rapidan
River

81

Madison
Run

Big Run

33

Trout Streams of Virginia
© 1999 The Countryman Press, Inc.

Below the swift stretch is a wide, deep pool, fed by silken water drop-ping over a low stone bench. The natives in here are somewhat larger than the usual Shenandoah Park inhabitants and are sturdy, well-fed fish. It's per-fect dry-fly water, and in the spring good action may be had on a number 14 Adams, or similar brown patterns.

If you come to the Shenandoah Park to fish, don't leave without giving Big Run a try. It's as near a wilderness experience as the park can offer. One caution: The flow is susceptible to summer drought, particularly lower down. Even though Big Run is indeed a big, boisterous stream just after the spring thaw, in midsummer the last couple of miles go underground.

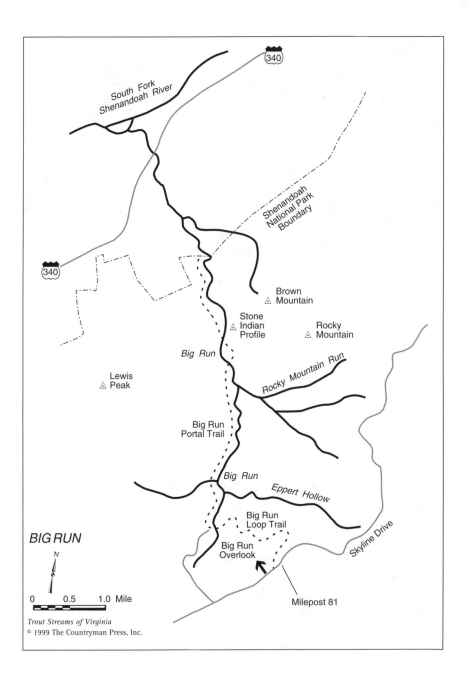

340

South Fork
Shenandoah River

Shenandoah
National Park
Boundary

340

Brown
△ Mountain

Stone
△ Indian
Profile

Rocky
△ Mountain

Big Run

Rocky Mountain Run

Lewis
△ Peak

Big Run
Portal Trail

Big Run

Eppert Hollow

Big Run
Loop Trail

Big Run
Overlook

Skyline Drive

Milepost 81

BIG RUN

N

0   0.5   1.0 Mile

Trout Streams of Virginia
© 1999 The Countryman Press, Inc.

Falls such as this one keep Shenandoah Park streams well oxygenated in the summer.

CONWAY RIVER / DEVIL'S DITCH

Stream Type Freestone

Maps USGS Fletcher; DeLorme 68

Access The primary access is VA(s) 667 through the town of Fletcher. Northbound from US 29, turn west onto US 33 to Stanardsville. There turn right onto VA(s) 230, for 3 miles, then left onto VA(s) 667, which parallels the Conway upstream into the Rapidan Wildlife Management Area, on past the intersection of Devil's Ditch.

This stream's upper reaches flow through the Shenandoah National Park, and the regulations governing the park's wild brook trout population apply. Lower down, the Conway and its major tributary, Devil's Ditch, lie within the Rapidan Wildlife Management Area.

The Conway River Road follows the stream for most of its length, providing easy access. A typical Shenandoah range fishery, it's an attractive stream, well worth a visit. It suffers during midsummer droughts but can be fished productively during the spring and fall, sometimes even well into December. Be prepared for a full day of stream-lashing on the Conway with firm regrets when dusk deepens enough to make even a parachute fly invisible. The light cahill hatch in May calls for a matching number 14 dry and nymph. The first major hatch here, as on most Shenandoah Park streams, is the quill gordon in March and April, calling for number 14 or 12 drys or nymphs. When fly hatches die down in summer and fall, keep a sharp eye for terrestrial fill-ins: crickets, hoppers, beetles, and both black and red ants.

Adult brook trout in the upper reaches range from 7 to 11 inches, on the average. There are healthy wild brown trout scattered through the lower reaches, with some occasional rod-benders exceeding 20 inches.

EAST HAWKSBILL CREEK

Stream Type Freestone

Maps USGS Big Meadows; DeLorme 74

Access This stream is reached from the Hawksbill Gap parking area, between Skyline Drive mileposts 45 and 46. The concrete marker at the trailhead indicates the lower Hawksbill Trail down the west side of the Shenandoah Range. Do not take this more heavily used footpath on the left. Go 20 feet to the right and follow that connector across the Appalachian Trail about 200 feet down. This connector trail then continues to a running water standpipe labeled SPRING. From there down to the stream a park ranger reported there is a wagon road. Good luck! The uppermost reaches of East Hawksbill, a spring branch, follow a mile-long rock slide at a 40-degree angle down, conjuring up the image of a potato wagon teetering over the brink and bouncing out of control three times to the bottom. There may be the trace of a wagon road several hundred yards to the right of the spring branch, but rainstorms and hurricanes have pretty well obliterated it. A safer bet is to follow the headwaters down to the point at which the Hawksbill begins to look like a trout stream.

For the mountain-stream purist who wants absolute solitude along with native trout fishing, the East Hawksbill has much to offer. Like most precious commodities, however, the rare solitude carries a high price. After descending the precipitous mountainside and fishing all day, you still have that teeth-clenching climb back to the top to reckon with. On the plus side, the stream is small enough to be fished without hip waders, so you don't need their added weight.

After navigating down the mountainside for about an hour, you hear the reassuring sound of falling water ahead, and through the trees you'll see the mini-waterfalls of the East Hawksbill. The stream's upper section offers few trout, so before assembling your fly-rod it's a good idea to hike down to where the gradient is a little gentler. Here there are more waterfalls and rapids, but with deeper green granite bowls beneath them containing more frequent trout shapes.

The rapid water discourages aquatic insects to some degree, but even in late October a small, hardy colony of mayflies has been spotted, looking a little wobbly at the prospect of being born into Indian summer. The usual terrestrials, number 16 red and black ants plus small beetles and black gnats, also may stir up some action. It's one of those streams with overhanging limbs through which you find a space to insert your rod, then dap the fly against a rock with a likely-looking dark shadow beneath it.

It's recommended that you time your fishing on the East Hawksbill to give you plenty of daylight for the trip back up the mountain. There's no public access at the lower end. It's also a good idea to have a companion with you, as much of the trail requires stepping from boulder to boulder, with the good possibility of a sprained ankle. Trekking to the East Hawksbill isn't easy by any standards, but then, you won't find any boot tracks or beverage cans along the stream. Even if you don't hook an abundance of trout, this may still become your most memorable fishing experience in the Shenandoah Park.

HUGHES RIVER

Stream Type Freestone

Maps USGS Old Rag Mountain; DeLorme 74

Access The best way to reach this stream is from above, between Skyline Drive mileposts 38 and 39. Park at the Stony Man Overlook and take the Nicholson Hollow Trail, which is 300 yards north of the parking area. This takes you 1.8 miles down the mountainside, over a feeder stream, and to the Hughes. Fishing is best at and below the Corbin Cabin.

The Hughes River can also be reached from below, by taking VA(s) 600 through the town of Nethers past the Old Rag Mountain parking area. About a mile farther is a small pull-off, and from there the Nicholson Hollow Trail follows the stream for the most part, occasionally straying away from the water. The upper stretch of this stream provides better action.

Fishing the Hughes River on a good day can fulfill the greatest expectations of Shenandoah native trout fishing. These are not large brookies, but they are scrappy and so colorful they look like cylindrical autumn maple leaves lying on the bottom. To dismiss these fish as too minuscule to be worthy is like dismissing Sugar Ray Leonard as too small to be a fighter. And occasionally there is the wily native heavyweight with lip scars to prove how many seasons he has survived.

The Hughes is a deceptive stream, with long shallow pools that seem devoid of life. But a black-bodied number 18 parachute fly dropped on these insignificant-looking flats can produce instant small explosions of red and gold. The farther downstream you fish, the bigger the water, with man-sized feeder streams along the way. Paradoxically, the larger fish, and more of them, seem to occur upstream all the way to the Corbin Cabin, a restored settler's home, identical to most Appalachian log originals still standing. This heavy upstream population may be due to less fishing pressure farther from the road. Since it's nearly 2 miles from the Skyline Drive, with a taxing uphill climb after fishing, the upper Hughes is not for everyone. Even those with a taste for solitary fishing should have had their annual physicals fairly recently. The Nicholson Hollow Trail is not a difficult walk, but it definitely is uphill all the way back, and steeply so at that.

A mile or so below the Corbin Cabin the gradient is steeper with fewer quiet pools, thus calling for slightly different tactics. A number 16 black ant, cast (intentionally) onto the side of a boulder and then coaxed into the rapids, closely approximates one feeding pattern. When these fish are hungry, however, almost anything that touches the water from any angle is attacked instantly. In the spring with active hatches about, Light Cahill or Hendrickson number 16s may attract more discriminating feeders.

Whatever the season, as with any native stream, delicate changes may make the difference. As an example, casting with a 5X leader, a perfectly respectable practice, may produce zero strikes. But changing to a number 6 or 7 leader on a given day may break the silence instantly. Believe it or not, switching from a black to a red ant fished dry can wake up dormant trout appetites. On these Shenandoah streams it is always a good idea to see what is flying or crawling and to turn over an underwater stone or two for a nymph check.

Regardless of the entomological population, a Muddler Minnow may turn the trick. Fishing for native trout on the Hughes, or anywhere for that matter, is seldom a predictable science, despite what merchandisers of fly-fishing equipment would have us believe. The river may have unstoppable action, with small red-and-gold thunderbolts striking at every pool, while only a few miles away, on a similar stream such as the Rose River, there's no sign of trout.

Since the Shenandoah is strictly a no-hunting park, you will sometimes get the distinct feeling you're being watched on the Hughes. A look across the river may disclose a doe grazing on the opposite bank, with only an occasional diffident glance at the odd human waving a 7½-foot sapling at the water.

Author's Note *On a summery October 4, I found myself on the Hughes River after an essentially fruitless morning on other streams in the Shenandoah Park. To my surprise, the colorful little Hughes River brookies smashed everything I offered them, wet or dry. I could do no wrong, and after releasing 20 autumnally crimson-and-gold brookies, I lost count. The farther upstream I moved, the more intense the action, which is often the case with these Shenandoah streams.*

The Hughes River offers good native trout fishing almost anytime, but it's a perfect stream for a warm late-autumn or Indian-summer day. It's not necessary to arrive early in the morning, and in fact at that time of the year midmorning may be better, with the water warming up and even some hardy hatches appearing. The one problem is confusion created by multicolored leaves floating downstream, making your fly more difficult to single out. Switching to wets can sometimes clear up the confusion. And the walk back up the mountainside on a brisk autumn evening is much less demanding than during the sweaty season.

MADISON RUN

Stream Type Freestone

Maps USGS Stanardsville; DeLorme 67

Access At the town of Grottoes, turn east off US 340 onto VA(s) 663, which takes you to the Shenandoah Park boundary, where the road is chained off. Walking is easy up this fire road through the park, with the stream visible on your right some of the way.

There is also access from the Skyline Drive up above, by parking at the Browns Gap area near milepost 83 and hiking down the Madison Run Road. Nevertheless, it is not recommended that you approach from the top, because the stream is too small to fish for nearly 5 miles down.

The impression one gets of Madison Run is of a gentle little stream, fairly level, and without the cabin-sized boulders found on most other Shenandoah Park streams. Rippling off the crest of the Shenandoah range, it is a rather small stream, dropping sharply down to Dundo Hollow. But after that, the gradient is very gentle in between Furnace and Austin Mountains. That lower stretch through the flats is a good place to take your grandfather fishing.

The Madison never increases much in size as it flows west and is very susceptible to dry weather. Even when there is adequate flow, the best pools are rather shallow, but they extend long enough for some easy 30-foot casts. Most of the wild trout caught are small, possibly because the easy access depletes the stream of keeper-sized fish. At this writing, brook trout 9 inches or longer are still being harvested here in the Shenandoah National Park. It is hoped that this killing regulation will change in the future, but in the meantime, conscientious anglers always catch and release these fragile little natives.

Like most of these little park streams, Madison Run offers some good dry-fly action on mayfly, caddis fly, and stonefly hatches until summer. Then something such as a size 16 Shenk's Cricket or other such terrestrial imitation is recommended.

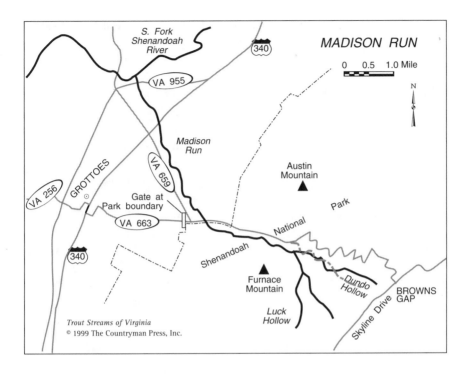

Trout Streams of Virginia
© 1999 The Countryman Press, Inc.

RAPIDAN RIVER

Stream Type Freestone

Maps USGS Fletcher; DeLorme 68

Special Regulations Below the bridge at Camp Hoover is catch-and-release water; fishing is restricted to artificial flies or lures with single hooks. (Note: Below the Shenandoah National Park boundary, barbed hooks are permitted.) All trout must be handled carefully and returned immediately to the water; possession of trout, of any size, is illegal. Game fish of other species may be kept, subject to regulations applying to various species in Virginia waters in general.

Access To reach the Camp Hoover stream access from the Skyline Drive, it is necessary to hike approximately 2 miles on a moderately difficult trail. Park at the Milam Gap area, between mileposts 52 and 53 of the Skyline Drive. Cross the highway and take the Appalachian Trail, blazed with white, which immediately intersects with Mill Prong Trail, blazed with blue. Follow that to the horse trail, where the blazes become yellow, leading past Big Rock Falls to Camp Hoover. Just below the camp where the Laurel and Mill Prongs join, regulated fishing on the Rapidan begins.

From below, access to the central portion of the Rapidan is via VA(s) 649/670 from Criglersville. The lower portion is reached by VA(s) 662 from

Graves Mill. The distance from the locked gate on the Rapidan Road to Camp Hoover is around a mile and a half.

Special restrictions on fishing (see "Special Regulations" above) have preserved a fair population of Rapidan brook trout, the smaller of which are easily seen. Larger fish are more wary and hook-wise, and the use of 6X leader is recommended, particularly at times of low water.

Hiking in to the Rapidan's headwaters at Camp Hoover from above takes around half an hour, most of it downhill. The perfectly preserved 60-year-old camp buildings are reserved for use by members of Congress and their staffs, some of whom emulate President Herbert Hoover, who loved to get away from Washington and fish for brook trout in the Rapidan. The president was said to have a "quick wrist"—certainly an asset, though not a necessity on this stair-step boulder-and-pool section of the stream. As you look down the mountainside, the stream is hidden by the chunks of granite marking its passage for a steep quarter of a mile. The hike in and out is part

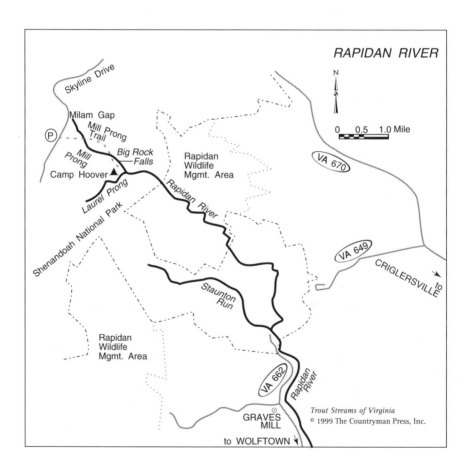

RAPIDAN RIVER

of the experience of fishing this historic stream, and you'i
deer from their fern beds or a family of wild turkeys cros

For the pure fly-fishing experience, the lower an
downstream may be reached by car. The ford connectin
es is tricky, however, and a high-clearance four-whe
save you from being stranded midstream miles from any pho...
ing, the ford and road are washed out in the lower section. The catcn-ա
release regulations also apply to the central and lower Rapidan.

Number 16 black beetles and dry ants, red or black, are productive.
There is also a rusty-colored fly called the Mr. Rapidan, tied locally in sizes
12 through 18, that is a warm-weather favorite. Hatches of reddish insects,
dead ringers for the Mr. Rapidan, may occasionally be seen flitting on the
surface. Depending on the time of year, nymphs, streamers, and hatch-
matched dry flies are successful.

ROSE RIVER

Stream Type Freestone

Maps USGS Big Meadows; DeLorme 68, 74

Access From the Skyline Drive, the stream is reached from Fisher's Gap
parking area by hiking down the Rose River Fire Road. The trail follows
most of the river down to the lower park boundary.

From below it may be reached from VA(s) 670, which at Banco branches off primary VA 231 north toward Criglersville. Route 670 ends at the
lower end of Rose River Fire Road, which is blocked to vehicles above the
park boundary. Parking here is at a premium because of the many hikers'
vehicles lining the road.

More deserving of the surname river than most other similarly labeled
Shenandoah Park streams, the Rose empties out of the park with a
respectable volume of water. Driving up VA(s) 670, you see stocking signs
along the way, with numerous spin-fishermen taking advantage of the easy
road access along the 100-foot-wide flow.

The tranquil nature of the stream ends as it flows down from the park
above. Up there it becomes the usual beautifully stair-stepped mountainside
fishery, offering deep holes among the boulders for native trout hideaways,
plus rapids above the drop-offs that should be productive. The stream bottom has the pale glow peculiar to some freestone streams.

The Rose River is one of the better-known Shenandoah Park streams,
probably because of its size. There are approximately 90 open trout fisheries
within the park boundaries, many quite small. "Approximately" applies
because, depending upon drought or fish population, various smaller streams

losed at times. It is a good idea to check on conditions with the park formation service, particularly during the summer. Native trout are the most precious and fragile resource within the preserve, and care is taken to prevent depletion.

> **Author's Note** *The Rose is a paradoxical stream. It's labeled a brook trout fishery and harbors some large specimens, but stories have filtered out of the Rose about big browns—18 inches or so—that are probably holdovers from stocked fish that have migrated upstream into native trout water. They are rare, but their foot-and-a-half-plus size has a way of jolting all preconceptions of brook trout fishing from your mind. The browns live here on borrowed time, since it is the policy of Shenandoah Park trout management to remove all but the native brook trout. Not everyone agrees with that policy. And although the few brown trout caught here are outsized, the wisdom of park management seems borne out by the disproportionately large heads of these browns, indicating inadequate food for such large specimens.*
>
> *Another of the Rose's paradoxes is its occasional drought of any angling action, despite ideal water conditions and plenty of trout shapes plainly visible, followed a day later by the same brookies eagerly flashing at a nymph from their dark stations beneath the deeply undercut boulders. Such fickle behavior is one of the perverse reasons fly-fishers keep coming back to the Shenandoah's native trout fisheries year after year.*

According to those who fish the Rose River frequently, caddis fly, mayfly, and stonefly hatches keep the surface action going well into June. After that, on a good day, terrestrials, and particularly small beetles, do well. However, there are no guarantees.

SMITH CREEK, ROCKINGHAM COUNTY

Stream Type Limestone

Maps USGS Broadway; DeLorme 73

Special Regulations Smith Creek has been purchased by a private individual and is currently scheduled to open as a pay-for-fish stream January 1, 2000.

Access Take exit 257 off I-81 to US 11 south. Go to Lacey Spring and turn east on VA(s) 806, then back north on VA(s) 986. Park at the gate.

Smith Creek, in Rockingham County, is not to be confused with the famous Smith River brown trout fishery in Franklin County. The creek begins with Lacey Springs, boiling up among the cress and other aquatic plants. It comes from the same limestone-water action that carved Luray Caverns and many similar caves in the vicinity. Flowing north, the regulated stretch passes through 100 percent pastureland with a gentle gradient.

Most of the way the west bank has been cut away about 6 feet, allowing one to approach the water unseen at a crouch. The upper stretch is bordered with bittersweet and brier bushes with the uncanny ability to snare any backcast. Lower down, the stream widens and there are cleared banks, making for textbook casts.

The downstream portion is surrounded by active cattle pasturage, and the animals have their run of the stream. This plus the warmer water lower down makes the upstream portion the more active fishery. In fact, back in the 1970s, the Inland Fisheries people branded Smith Creek "borderline" because of the higher water temperatures downstream. This has changed, perhaps because of the additional overhanging tree growth now shading the stream more completely.

For someone who grew up in western Virginia, Smith Creek brings to mind childhood memories of farm streams usually called "branches" or "cricks." On a Sunday afternoon the farmer might rise out of his leather easy chair long enough to take a city kid down to the pasture. There with a birch pole and nightcrawler, batches of "hornyheads" would be agitated out of their Sabbath rest. And occasionally there would be the thrill of color flashing when a brookie was hauled out from underneath a small waterfall. The farmer would hold the scarlet-and-silver fish for a moment and then release it back into the crick to be caught another Sunday.

Smith Creek is a larger version of that childhood crick, with brown trout instead of brook, plus some decent rainbows. When asked what flies to use early in the year, Ken Puckett recommended Chironomid Midges, numbers 20–22, presumably with a 2-pound leader. Mr. Puckett is the Trout Unlimited member largely responsible for advancing Smith Creek's trout management to its present state. Up near Lacey Springs some smaller rainbows actively feed among the clusters of aquatic plants. Farther downstream their larger relatives are occasionally hooked.

During warmer weather an Adams number 18 can be an effective attractor. Later in the summer, when grasshoppers abound in the meadow, the Letort Hopper dry and Shenks Cricket dry are the most effective lures on the Smith as well as most Virginia spring creeks.

Smith Creek has become an excellent brown trout fishery, although it will probably never achieve the status of Mossy Creek because of its higher water temperature and use by cattle. The latter could change. As it stands, Smith Creek is an easy place to while away a warm spring afternoon in a most pleasant manner along with the browns and resident colony of Canada geese.

WHITEOAK CANYON RUN

Stream Type Freestone

Maps USGS Old Rag Mountain; DeLorme 74

Access To avoid confusion, be aware that some old-timers still refer to Whiteoak Canyon Run as Robinson River. The most convenient park entry to this stream is from the Limberlost Parking Area on the east side of Skyline Drive at milepost 43. A tenth-of-a-mile hike down Old Rag Fire Road leads to Whiteoak Canyon Trail. This clearly marked, gentle pathway takes you to the stream and continues all the way to the falls and the bottom of the mountain. To reach it from the bottom, you can drive in on VA(s) 600 to streamside and follow Whiteoak Canyon Trail up from there.

This is a stream of superlatives, and although everyone has his best trout water, Whiteoak Canyon Run is the favorite of more than a few. A visiting stream-lasher from Arizona or New Mexico, or even eastern Oregon, may be excused for his questioning of the so-called poverty belt of the Appalachians upon taking his first look at Whiteoak Canyon Run. For the westerner, these millions of gallons of cold, pure water from the Appalachian aquifer are a treasure as precious as diamonds.

Although not the most productive Shenandoah Park stream, it may be enjoyed purely as a trout fishery, with no need to look farther than the dazzling native trout, some of them reaching a foot and longer. Or the trout-seeker with a taste for entomology can be occupied full-time observing the frequent mayfly, caddis fly, and stonefly hatches. Hikers take the Whiteoak Canyon Trail purely for the beauty of the stream and the virgin hemlocks along its banks.

Before fishing here the first time, it's a good idea to walk in from above and see the stream's beginning, starting with fingers of water in a shining creep across the top of the ground. The fingers suddenly all converge with a roar into a fist, making a mature stream with holes 10 feet deep or better. Next take a hike below the falls and look back up at the total volume reached. There is a bolt of white water roaring through an 80-foot granite chute, falling to the valley floor below. Even the most intrepid French kayaker would be unable to make it through this chute in one piece—without a parachute. With a full appreciation of the stream's personality, you can fish it with an even more complete enjoyment.

Waders are a must here, as is a complete assortment of number 16 or 18 dry flies and nymphs. Accessible as they are, the native brookies have a habit of coming up for a close look at your lure and then turning disdainfully away. Or what is even more disquieting, they strike the blood knot in your leader. This is a sure sign that a 6X or (seriously) 7X leader is what

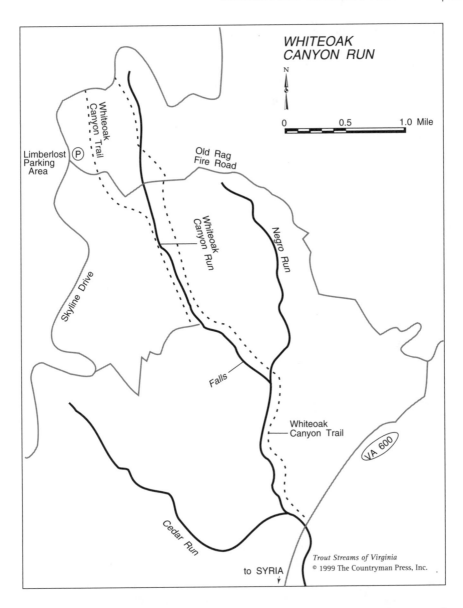

WHITEOAK
CANYON RUN

N

0   0.5   1.0 Mile

Whiteoak Canyon Trail

Limberlost
Parking
Area

Old Rag
Fire Road

Whiteoak
Canyon Run

Negro Run

Skyline Drive

Falls

Whiteoak
Canyon Trail

VA 600

Cedar Run

to SYRIA

Trout Streams of Virginia
© 1999 The Countryman Press, Inc.

they prefer, tied to the smallest fly you can manage. The usual tactics of staying low, using all available camouflage and cover, and going slow apply emphatically on this stream. Casual fishing will produce an abundance of near-fingerling-sized brook trout, but the heavy hitters can only be enticed from their rock hideaways with extreme care and some skill.

One Blue Ridge Parkway–dwelling fisherman favors log-walking as a method of approaching the more canny larger fish without being spotted. There are huge hemlock logs frequently acting as bridges high above the channel. Easing out onto one of them and casting upstream will occasionally catch a hungry brookie by surprise.

Be prepared to make a day of it. And be prepared for dazzling surroundings. You'll be tempted to cast a fly into every enticing piece of tailwater along Whiteoak Canyon Run.

3 | Alleghany Highlands

Bordered to the north by Highland County, this area is where the great east-ern rivers, the Potomac and James, begin before any hint of pollution is felt. Highland County lists its population at around 3,000—fewer people than in the 1930s and only one-fifth as many as the present sheep population. No such census of trout is available, but it is a safe bet that the rainbows out-number the people here. Highland has the highest mean elevation east of the Mississippi, averaging heights of all the county's peaks. This explains why there was never a railroad through it and why the hardwood timber coun-try has remained primarily an outdoor recreational paradise.

Just south of Highland is Bath County, where the Jackson River becomes one of the state's big-water trout streams in Hidden Valley. Below Gathright Dam in Alleghany County, the lower Jackson is rapidly becoming one of the most talked-about trout fisheries in the state. Above the dam, Lake Moomaw is stocked regularly with brown and lake-run rainbow trout, along with a number of warm-water species. The shoreline is adjacent to the 13,428-acre T. M. Gathright Wildlife Management Area, under the supervision of the Virginia Department of Game and Inland Fisheries. Although all native game species are managed and produced here, the specialty is wild turkey.

Funded by the federal government, the Gathright Dam impoundment serves a number of purposes, the most relevant being improvement of water quality in the upper Jackson River by increasing its flow during periods of drought. The greater flow of cool water raises oxygen levels and washes away stagnant pools, creating ideal conditions for trout spawning and growth. An added plus for those launching a canoe at one of the six author-ized ramps—the consistent water level has enhanced what was already a beautiful streamside vista.

This area generally contains the state's really big trout waters—the

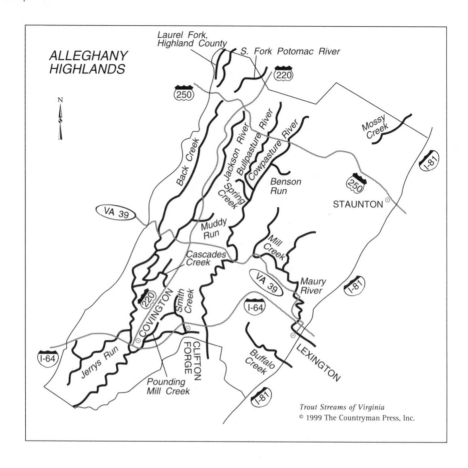

ALLEGHANY HIGHLANDS

Laurel Fork, Highland County

S. Fork Potomac River

Bullpasture River

Cowpasture River

Jackson River

Back Creek

Spring Creek

Mossy Creek

Benson Run

STAUNTON

VA 39

Muddy Run

Mill Creek

Cascades Creek

Maury River

Smith Creek

COVINGTON

Jerrys Run

CLIFTON FORGE

Pounding Mill Creek

Buffalo Creek

LEXINGTON

Trout Streams of Virginia
© 1999 The Countryman Press, Inc.

Jackson, Bullpasture, and Maury Rivers, for example. Here there is plenty of room for a big loop of backcast without snagging a limb. On the other hand, a little bushwhacking can lead to some public lands containing very private smaller wild trout streams, such as Benson Run. The more adventurous take note: Snagging a tough rhododendron leaf is the order of the day on these rugged little Alleghany Highlands waters.

BACK CREEK

Stream Type Primarily limestone, some freestone

Maps USGS Mountain Grove, Sunrise; DeLorme 65

Special Regulations Upstream of Mountain Grove is a short stretch of delayed harvest regulated fishing, single-hook, artificial lures, with a limit of two trout over 16 inches. These waters are maintained by the Virginia Electric Power Company as part of their Bath County Pumped Storage Station Recreation Area. Be prepared for a stream that looks a little as though it might have been designed by the Corps of Engineers, with chiseled stone ripraps forming the banks.

Access Turn west off US 220 onto VA 39 west. Cross Back Creek Mountain into the George Washington National Forest. Turn left at the sign reading BLOWING SPRINGS CAMPGROUND. To reach the special-regulations stretch, turn right from VA 39 onto VA(s) 600 at Hiner's store and proceed north to the recreation area entrance.

B ack Creek is a sizable stream, by Virginia mountain standards, with deep rapids requiring chest waders for full coverage. Driving into the Blowing Springs Campground area, you may park at the entrance to a road closed to vehicles, which puts you within easy walking distance of good fishing on Back Creek.

West of Blowing Springs, VA 39 parallels Back Creek upstream, with frequent gravel turnoffs. From these there are well-traveled paths leading down to the deeper holes. This is a signal that the less heavily fished areas are away from these beaten paths. What many do not realize is that the larger fish are lying in the rapids or small potholes between them.

Were it not next to a busy highway leading into West Virginia, complete with 18-wheelers, Back Creek might see fewer weekend anglers. Midweek, the traffic tends to die down, particularly as hot weather arrives in June. Downstream from Blowing Springs, the stream departs from the highway

The author fishes on a regulated stretch of Back Creek.

into an area called Back Creek Gorge, reached by a walking trail only. This eases the fishing pressure slightly. Farther down there seems to be a run of McGahey rainbows migrating up from Lake Moomaw, providing a special kind of fishing.

Near Blowing Springs is a gauging station operated by the Virginia Division of Water Resources. The information recorded there is used to measure the amount of water drained from Back Creek's 131 square miles of watershed. During one decade the recorded maximum flow was 65,450 gallons per second. Above the gauging station the stream is crossed by a concrete bridge, where the sign indicates BIG BACK CREEK. The old bridge abutment still remains, and where it projects into the stream is a likely hideout for a big brown or two. Just past the bridge, posted land begins and continues to the village of Mountain Grove, where Little Back Creek merges with the main stream.

The headwaters hold brook and rainbow trout, while downstream is dominated by browns and rainbows. Brook trout are more prevalent north of the Highland–Bath county line. There are excellent spring mayfly hatches all along the stream, including quill gordons and march browns. Winter stoneflies are present into early spring. The most consistently effective attractor fly is the Adams number 14 or 16, along with Wulffs and hair wings.

BENSON RUN

Stream Type Freestone

Maps USGS Deerfield; DeLorme 65

Access Williamsville, unlike Williamsburg, is not a readily recognized Virginia landmark, consisting as it does of a post office, abandoned store, and not much else. From VA 39 just west of Millboro Springs, look for the sign where VA(s) 678 turns north. Follow it to the outskirts of Williamsville, where the road forks right to a concrete bridge across the Cowpasture River. This is VA(s) 614, which becomes a gravel road just past the firehouse. Follow 614 a couple of miles to a high cut in the road looking down on the confluence of Benson Run with the Cowpasture. Down at the bottom of the cut there is a farmhouse that has been converted into the Benson Run Hunt Club. Turn in there and look for the gate, which you should close behind you. Ford the stream and begin the stretch of rugged roadway that takes you to some fine brook trout fishing.

For the less adventurous, there are two additional access routes. One is FR 173, which turns to the west off of VA(s) 629 approximately 2 miles north of the town of Deerfield. The other is a spur off FR 394 known as the Sugar Tree Road. This is reached by following VA(s) 614 as above, turning to the right at the SUGAR TREE sign a couple of miles before reaching Benson Run, and driving up the mountain to a spur on the left designated FR 394B. From the dead end it's a short hike to the fishing area.

If there were a T-shirt reading I RODE THE ROAD TO BENSON RUN—AND SURVIVED, it could be worn with pride by a very special cadre of trout fishermen. When you mention this stream to the older generation of hardy anglers, their eyes glaze over as they say things like, "Yeah, I was up there in '51. Lost my exhaust pipe on that @#!!! road."

As you enter the road to Benson Run, you will see the U.S. Department of Agriculture sign with the word GATE chiseled in the wood and hung on—you guessed it—a gate. Farther up the mountain there is the usual yellow diamond sign reading ROUGH ROAD. If there ever were an award for under-statement, this sign would win without question. The single-lane road climbs abruptly and then swings down off the mountain into a floodplain. Here is where the springs of your vehicle, along with your tailbone, get a thumping from the potholes.

Occasionally it is necessary to dodge around a fresh-cut tree stump in the middle of the road. Attempting to ride above the ruts, you slide into them frequently because there's no shoulder. Then there is a 6-foot drop-off where floods have taken out a section of the road. At this point it becomes necessary to strike out through the woods between trees far enough apart to accommodate both fenders. After about an hour of this, most of it at 5 miles per hour, Benson Run begins to look more and more fishable, and it's time to find a space wide enough to park your four-wheel drive. (Don't drive to Benson Run in anything less!)

Approaching the stream, you are impressed most by the cathedral-like quality of the huge hemlocks on the floodplain, which let slices of sunlight through. The quiet is absolute, except for the sighing of the stream and per-haps a pileated woodpecker at work. Situated on a mountain plateau, Ben-son Run is not one of the boisterous, roaring spring streams usually found in this area. It flows beyond a number of alternate beds, now dry, cut by Hurricane Hugo in 1989. The banks are around 4 feet high and closely held by hemlock and pine trees. Casting a fly requires some patience, and it helps to take a deep breath and a careful look at the network of limbs above a pool before making the first cast to it.

There are a couple of requirements for the trip to Benson Run. First, have a four-wheel-drive vehicle in good condition. If it fails on you at the end of the road, there's quite a hike out to get help. Second, be prepared to bounce arrhythmically, as there's no pattern to the potholes and rocks in the roadway to Benson Run. And third, be assured that the trip will be worth-while. There's so little adventure left in the lower eastern United States that sometimes it goes unrecognized or is mistaken for discomfort and inconvenience. There's plenty of both on the trip up to Benson Run, but there's a biting edge of adventure about it as well.

BUFFALO CREEK

Stream Type Limestone

Maps USGS Glasgow; DeLorme 53

Special Regulations From the confluence of Collier's Creek upstream 2.9 miles to the confluence of North and South Buffalo Creeks, fishing is restricted to single-hook artificial lures; creel limit two fish per day; all trout less than 16 inches long must be handled carefully and returned unharmed to the water; possession of trout less than 16 inches long on this water is illegal; trespassing in areas marked as fish sanctuaries is illegal; camping, alcoholic beverages, firearms, swimming, fires, and picnicking are prohibited; wading is permitted; access must be at designated parking and fence-crossing points. Written permission to fish is needed, as this water is private property; the landowner's rights must be respected, and failure to do so may result in loss of fishing privileges. Permission slips may be obtained at the Virginia Game and Inland Fisheries Verona office, or from the landowner's home at streamside.

Access Take VA 251 west off US 11, just south of Lexington. Follow 251 to VA(s) 612 and turn south. Route 612 follows the stream in a southerly direction and offers one designated parking area and a number of other places where you can pull off the road, adjacent to some of the best fishing stretches.

A careful approach to the deep pool just above the footbridge at the downstream end of the special-regulations section may give you your first clue as to what kind of trout stream the Buffalo is. Often there are brown trout lying next to the bank ranging in length from 18 to 24 inches. If you are fortunate enough to spot these giants, it won't be for long. They soon disappear to parts unknown and are very fickle about coming out to take flies. This same stretch is the scene of much frenzied surface feeding.

From the footbridge at the only parking area to a sign downstream reading TROUT SANCTUARY, there is no fishing allowed. The Buffalo describes an 180-degree loop about the landowner's home, and he has courteously requested that the loop be designated a sanctuary to protect his privacy. So although no real fish-management purpose is served by the sanctuary, it shelters a permanently undisturbed population of trout.

Buffalo Creek is formed by the confluence of two limestone-spring streams and is fed along the way by numerous other smaller springs, guaranteeing a good summer flow. Along its low to moderate gradient are several textbook pools and many large, deep flats. Below the sanctuary, the last mile of regulated stream cuts through a gorge dominated by large boulders and bedrock ledges. The footing is more slippery in the gorge, and additional care should be used when wading.

The usual hatches in this area can be imitated by a Ginger Quill number 14, Adams 16, Light Cahill 16, or Dark Hendrickson 14. When all else fails, small terrestrials such as black and cinnamon ants may be productive.

Just about any time of day you can see surface activity, but don't be misled. Despite all the pops and splashes, these fish give new meaning to the word *wary*. They have seen more fly and leader combinations than Rat-Faced MacDougal and will continue to feed inches away from your Light Cahill or Ginger Quill deceivers.

Another challenge on the Buffalo is the thick overhang of young maples, sycamores, and alders. These require most casts to be made from midstream, and even there it helps to roll-cast frequently. In other words, Buffalo Creek is a stream that truly tests your fly-fishing ability. You may do everything right: stalking the 2-footers from downstream, making a perfect cast, laying out your hatch-match just above their noses, double-hauling what little slack may have been left from your feather light drop. And with all that, you may finish a day on the Buffalo with pleasant memories of everything except that line-parting tug that only a citation brown can give.

BULLPASTURE RIVER

Stream Type Limestone

Maps USGS Monterey, Williamsville; DeLorme 65

Access The Bullpasture River is virtually 100 percent accessible by vehicle from VA(s) 678 all the way to Williamsville. Deep in the gorge are some stretches that demand a little extra legwork, which consequently aren't as heavily fished as the roadside holes. One such example is a series of parallel rock shelves that stretch between steep banks. The troughs between these shelves are deep enough to make chest waders a must but can usually be relied on for trout action any time of the year.

The name of this river, Bullpasture, and its course, flowing into the Cowpasture, conjures a quiet, flat stream meandering through pastureland. Nothing could be farther from the truth along the 5.5 miles of public trout water. This spectacular stream rises in Highland County, where the sheep population far outnumbers the human. It was named by early settlers for the numerous eastern buffalo that watered there, wearing deep trails that are moss-covered but still visible along the bank two centuries later.

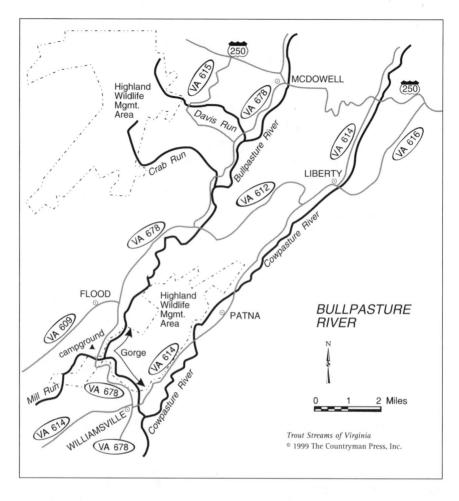

BULLPASTURE
RIVER

N

0   1   2 Miles

Trout Streams of Virginia
© 1999 The Countryman Press, Inc.

The upper stretch is mostly privately owned, posted against fishing, and indeed does run through comparatively flat cattle-grazing land for a short distance. Then a few miles above Williamsville, the Bullpasture takes a sudden drop through a rugged, wooded canyon called "the gorge." Looking remarkably like a western river, it tumbles against cabin-sized boulders, forming deep pools that hold trout throughout the summer months. Frequent cold springs feed into this gorge sector, giving the water an icy freshness even in July and August. Maintained by the state game commission, the gorge area fills the eye with hemlocks marching a thousand feet down the side of Bullpasture Mountain plus a parade of wildlife to distract one's concentration from a drifting Adams or Cahill.

Deer, wild turkeys, mink, wildcats, and otters may cause some of the shadows moving along the bank. But don't expect all to be pristine wilderness. The Bullpasture is stocked water and has been one of Virginia's most successful put-and-take streams since the state's trout-stocking program began. Rainbow, brown, and brook trout are provided regularly, and an attempt was even made at one time to start a population of Bitterroot browns, which failed. It was theorized that the 6-inch Bitterroot fingerlings were outcompeted by the larger fish already in place.

Above the gorge a small spring creek called Mill Run empties in, and at its mouth there is a public campground that tends to be crowded during the peak trout season. Called by some the number-one Virginia trout stream, the Bullpasture is well publicized and tends to be heavily populated with spin-fishermen. One way to get away from a weekend crowd is to explore the many spring creeks, such as Mill Run and Davis Run, in the vicinity of the Bullpasture. These creeks hold small but lively wild rainbows that must be stalked carefully and then tempted with a fly dangled 3 or 4 feet from your rod tip.

The author nets a brown on one of the rare placid stretches of the Bullpasture.

Finding these little gems may take some exploring, and you can be sure no self-respecting native trout angler will tell you about his favorite spring creek. But the effort of searching is well worth it. One should not be dismayed at the number of spin-casters and other competitors. The wilier fish, particularly browns, have plenty of room to elude them in the average 25-foot width of the Bullpasture, and there are multitudes of deep hiding holes beneath the rocks where a nymph or Muddler Minnow can be dangled with good success.

Another way of escaping the crowd is winter fishing the Bullpasture, at the risk of taking a header into 3 feet of pure, ice-rimmed misery. Even in January trout are active in Virginia, and some nice holdover fish may be taken. Because of the water volume of the Bullpasture, wilier fish elude the fair-weather anglers. The Virginia trout season lasts throughout the year, with stocking during the winter, but it doesn't hurt to have a white oak fire crackling in a nearby fireplace when wading at near-freezing air temperatures.

During any season the key to choosing the right fly for the Bullpasture is versatility. Be prepared with a good assortment of dry flies, plus some wets and nymphs for the many rapids and holes beneath small waterfalls. An all-around good choice is the Adams number 16, but it's advisable to check the Bullpasture hatches, as they change frequently. Sampling the duns can give a clue to those whirls of activity just under the surface. An opaque, flush-floating terrestrial such as a flying ant, Gypsy Moth, or Jassid may do the trick in late spring or summer. Sometimes you may spot green inchworms dropping from the many overhanging limbs, and adding an artificial greenie is sure to stir up the hungry mayhem.

Among the less encouraging sights in the Bullpasture are flashes of silver from the bellies of fish working the bottom. Examining the stomach contents of a brown deep-hooked amid such activity may reveal a handful of small black snail shells, for which there is no artificial counterpart. But the amateur entomologist should be prepared for myriad such invertebrate surprises brimming over in this exciting stream and go with the flow.

CASCADES CREEK

Stream Type Limestone

Maps USGS Healing Springs; DeLorme 52

Fees and Regulations Rods, reels, and lines are for rent at the Cascades Inn, and flies and accessories are for sale. The permit to fish is $40 per day.

Fishermen must have a Virginia state fishing license or trip-fishing license, valid for 5 successive days. State residents pay $5.50 for trip licenses, while nonresidents are charged $6.50. All licenses are available at the Cascades Inn. The private permit specifies that only fishing with flies is authorized. Many prefer to release all fish, but in some cases Homestead guests turn their catches over to the hotel chef for presentation at dinner that evening.

Access Drive US 220 north to the Homestead Hotel at Hot Springs and go to the Outpost Cottage Store. For advance information call 540-839-5355 or 703-839-5442.

As you descend from the Homestead's Cascades Inn down a gravel road to the stream, the elevation drops more than 800 feet. It becomes obvious that this is a different sort of environment altogether from that of the high ground. There is a celebration of life in this water-rich gorge, both animal and plant. The stream is surrounded by close to 16,000 acres of private land, much of it virgin forest.

On the rock cliff above the stream there are jack-in-the-pulpits with overleafs the size of a small girl's hand. Rare bloodred trilliums abound, along with wild orchids and scarlet columbines. One has the feeling that there must be some brilliantly colored rainbows beneath the surface of these

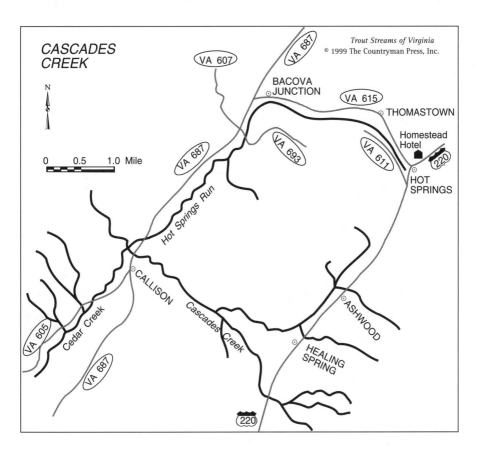

Beaver Shriver is a Cascades guide and proprietor of the Outpost fly shop.

pools to match all this glory above, and that is truly the case.

This 3-mile stretch of privately stocked and maintained stream is the domain of Beaver Shriver, who acts as guide for those lucky enough to discover the Cascades. He can identify the 10 or 12 varieties of nymphs revealed on an overturned stone and hand you his "secret weapon," a Light Cahill spinner fly he tied that morning. He can then introduce you to the hefty rainbow waiting just where he knows it will be, ready to smash his spinner. Afterward Beaver can demonstrate his technique of using forceps to remove the hook, releasing the trout without touching it.

You have your choice of a guided or solo trip. The experienced fly-angler may wish to explore the Cascades on his own, starting at the downstream end where there are startlingly clear pools for sharpshooting at rises with dry flies. Moving up, one encounters the falls that give the stream its name. These are seldom-stocked waters, with wild rainbows in the lees and eddies beneath frequent waterfalls. It takes a little hand-over-handing up stone cliffs to reach the pools, but the effort is worth it. Where the stone has been pounded by falling water for several millennia, the plunge pools are deep, as may be expected. Here a weighted nymph or Muddler is appropriate, despite Beaver's persuasion as a dry-fly purist.

In the Homestead tradition, novice fly-fishers will be treated with the same courtesy and respect as seasoned stream-lashers. A fishing pro is available at the Cascades Inn from 8 to 9 AM and 1 to 2 PM daily. After that he may be reached at the stream. For early-morning fishing, it is advisable to make arrangements the night before. Fly-fishing lessons are conducted on the stream for first-timers or seasoned anglers who wish to polish their technique.

The Cascades experience may not be for everyone, but there is nothing artificial about it. In no way does it resemble fishing a manicured English meadow stream. On the contrary, it is wilder and relatively untouched compared to most other Virginia trout waters.

JACKSON RIVER

Stream Type Limestone

Maps USGS Warm Springs, Falling Spring; DeLorme 64, 65

Access From US 220 turn west on VA 39, go about 3 miles to VA(s) 621, and turn north on 621 to the Hidden Valley Recreation Area. Follow VA(s) 621 for about a mile and then turn left onto VA(s) 615. After 1.5 miles you will reach the Hidden Valley Recreation Area. There is a camping section to the left with well-manicured facilities and a parking area straight ahead.

The Jackson is one of western Virginia's primary waterways, and this chapter concentrates upon only one small section of it, the Hidden Valley Recreation Area. For trout fishermen who need relief from the precious gem–like cascades and grottoes of Virginia's small mountain streams, the Jackson is relatively big water, at least in western Virginia terms. It is around 100 feet across at Hidden Valley, and at times much wider. There are riffles punctuated by long stretches of quiet water ideal for dry-fly fishing. Beginning in late April, fish may be seen rising there nearly every evening. There is excellent holdover brown fishing throughout Hidden Valley. And even though the Jackson does not have the immensity of some trout streams in Wyoming, say, or New Hampshire, or even Pennsylvania, none of those states has Virginia bluebells growing upon its stream banks in May.

To the first-time fisher of Hidden Valley, the most striking sight is the Warwick House across the river. It is a pre–Civil War mansion, its four massive Ionic columns still intact after nearly two centuries. This imposing dwelling could very well have been the home of Scarlett O'Hara's Virginia cousins, though appropriately enough it is now being remodeled as a bed & breakfast catering to trout anglers.

Even farther back in the history of this area, George Washington inspected the forts along the Jackson in 1755. It's tempting to speculate that the young George might have taken the time to cut a hickory sapling and try

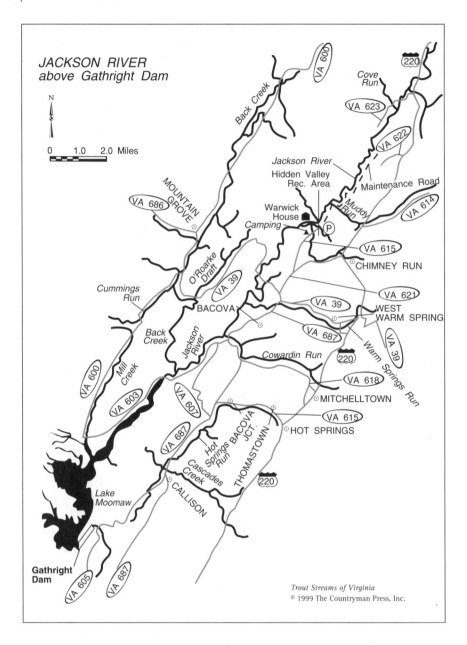

JACKSON RIVER
above Gathright Dam

N

0   1.0   2.0 Miles

Trout Streams of Virginia
© 1999 The Countryman Press, Inc.

his luck with the native brook trout with which the stream was packed during that century.

To fish the most productive site along the Jackson River, one must first walk about 3 miles up a maintenance road on which no motorized traffic is allowed. Although this does not seem a long distance, the road is scattered with heelless athletic socks eaten away by the chafing of waders. The combination of waders, socks, and 3 miles of road, level though it is, can be destructive. One ingenious father and his young son were observed riding bicycles with fly-rods strapped to their handlebars. This was one solution to the distance problem. Another would be to shoulder your waders and wear a good pair of walking shoes as far as the swinging bridge. Above the swinging bridge there is a 3-mile stretch of special-regulations fishing.

As part of the Jackson River fishing experience, Muddy Run is worth including. Upstream almost to the swinging bridge, this small stream flows into the Jackson from the east. It is not muddy at all but has a perpetually milky appearance from the mineral content of the soil through which it flows. A hefty population of wild rainbows can be roused from beneath its banks with a streamer or timely nymph. There is a marked trail following Muddy Run upstream until posted property is reached. It's a good sidebar trip away from the Jackson if the river trout aren't biting, or if your addictions tend toward Virginia's string of smaller watery gems gracing the state's western mountains.

JACKSON RIVER TAILWATER

Stream Type Limestone

Maps USGS Redwood; DeLorme 52

Special Regulations Live bait is permitted in the tailwater, and four trout per day over 12 inches may be creeled.

Release Information The Corps of Engineers maintains a recorded telephone message giving daily release information on the Jackson tailwater: 703-965-4117. As a general rule, any release less than 500 cubic feet per second (cfs) is wadable near the dam. Farther downstream can still be fished when the discharge is greater than 500 cfs. No real danger is posed by higher releases, but footing is trickier and water levels are less comfortable.

Access To reach Gathright Dam, turn west off US 220 between Covington and Hot Springs onto VA(s) 687. Cross the Jackson River at Petticoat Junction public access and proceed to where VA(s) 641 intersects. Take 641 west a short distance and turn right (north) on VA(s) 666. Then turn right on VA(s) 605 and follow it past the Morris Hill Campground. On the right there is a sign designating the fishing area. Turn right at the sign and follow the short lane that curves down to streamside and dead-ends just below the dam. This is the first public access. It is advised that you use only the six public access points, paying particular attention to the NO TRESPASSING signs above the Johnson Spring Access number 2.

The first cold-water release from Gathright Dam was in 1989, making this a relatively new Virginia tailwater. Fishing here is spectacular, especial-

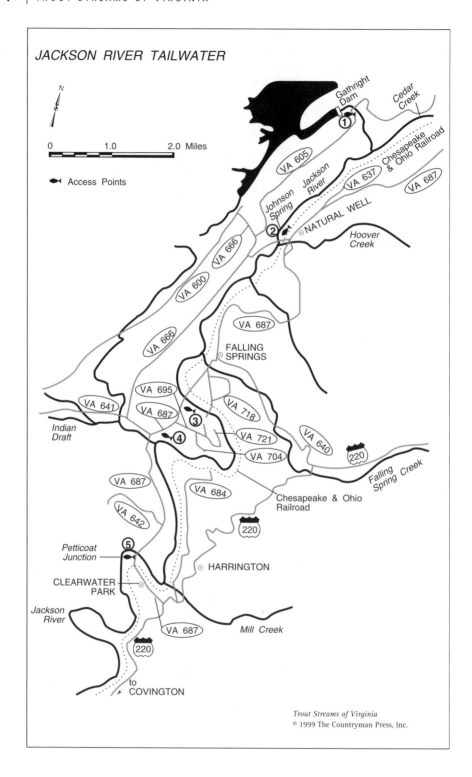

JACKSON RIVER TAILWATER

N

0   1.0   2.0 Miles

➤ Access Points

Gathright Dam

Cedar Creek

①

Chesapeake & Ohio Railroad

VA 605

Johnson Spring

Jackson River

VA 637

VA 687

② NATURAL WELL

Hoover Creek

VA 666

VA 600

VA 687

FALLING SPRINGS

VA 666

VA 695

VA 718

VA 641

VA 687

Indian Draft

③

VA 721

VA 640

④

VA 704

220

VA 687

VA 684

Falling Spring Creek

Chesapeake & Ohio Railroad

VA 642

220

Petticoat Junction ⑤

CLEARWATER PARK

HARRINGTON

Jackson River

VA 687

Mill Creek

220

to COVINGTON

Trout Streams of Virginia
© 1999 The Countryman Press, Inc.

ly in the upper section just below the dam. This 400- to 500-meter section was formerly the most popular of the seven public accesses, and on any weekend it was common to see 15 to 20 fly-fishermen stationed along the stream, plus a few bait-dunkers. Nowadays the 7 miles downstream is no longer open for fishing.

The average summer water temperature just below the dam is 59 degrees. In winter, when the surrounding water approaches 32 degrees, the dam release temperature ranges between 39 and 41 degrees. There are many ideal feeding stations in this upper stretch, producing some really big rainbows and browns, with the fastest growth rate on the river. An occasional citation fish will find its way from Lake Moomaw through the dam to the tailwater below. Because there is no power-generation system, and therefore no turbine blades, trout can come through unscathed. One example was a 2-foot tiger trout, a brown-brook crossbreed caught in 1992, the origin of which no one could quite figure out.

The regulated water temperatures have led to an interesting insect population. At any time of the year there can be midge hatches in the upper tailwater, particularly spectacular in early January. The most abundant of these are the order Diptera, which are the true flies. (To put it into plainer words, these are what most fishermen know as the gnats that fly into your eye just as you're making the final elusive loop in your blood knot.)

In the fall of 1990 and the winter of 1991, several knowledgeable anglers observed surface feeding on heavy fly hatches. Curious, they netted some of the insects and discovered they were immature blackfly larvae. Harry Steeves, a biology professor at Virginia Polytechnic Institute, delivered a sample of these to Steve Hiner at the Department of Entomology at Virginia Tech. They were confirmed to be genus *Simulium,* species *vittatum.* Steeves developed a fly pattern (Diptera) based on the specimens, and it is now commonly used below the Gathright Dam.

As a follow-up, Hiner and Steeves later developed an emerger pattern imitating the adult blackfly rising to the surface in an air bubble. After trying several unsuccessful materials, the team finally settled on clear plastic beads. From being virtually unknown, these blackfly designs have become commonly used patterns at the Gathright, not because these minute flies are easy to fish, but rather because they accurately duplicate the trout's everyday fare.

It became clear that there were stacked pods of sizable fish below the dam feeding on the thousands of blackfly larvae on the bottom, the same larvae that produced the bubble-enclosed adults at the surface. The hatch is not always heavy, but it is consistent. Just about every day of the year you can observe trout rising to blackflies at some time or other.

As for the 18 miles of tailwater downstream, the insect population is still changing in this relatively new fishery. The species mix is constantly

Fred Webb fishes into one of the many hatches along the Jackson River tailwater.

adjusting to the temperature regulation that began in 1989, heading toward one or two predominant mayfly and caddis fly species. This has been the historical insect pattern at newly established tailwaters, where most of the time the stronger flies take hold and become abundant, creating excellent hatches for the fly-angler. It is also possible that certain niches of the river will develop their own unique mix of fly hatches. This will be due to the differing belts of water temperature as you progress downstream. Steve Hiner anticipates a virtual supermarket of hatches, varying according to the distance from the regulated temperature at the release point. But it is certain that blackflies will continue to dominate immediately below the dam.

In order to avoid embarrassment, and perhaps even prosecution, anglers should be aware of the landowners' bans along the lower Jackson tailwater. Prior to building the dam, the Corps of Engineers agreed to furnish Virginia anglers a cold-water fishery. In anticipation of heavy public usage, the Corps purchased six access points along the riverbank. They also built a multi-million-dollar release tower for taking water out of the impoundment from various depths in order to control temperature below the dam. The river evolved from a warm-water fishery producing primarily chain pickerel and smallmouth and rock bass. In 1989 brown and rainbow trout were planted and immediately began to flourish. Wading and float fishermen converged on the area, along with recreational rafters and canoers. Five of the six access points were deeded to the U.S. Forest Service. Access is now under George Washington National Forest jurisdiction.

In the beginning there were few problems with landowners. But then several of them above Access Number 2 began to complain loudly. They wished to ban the public from the river bordered by their property, claiming that crown grants from King George III deeded to them the river bottom and all resources above. This included the trout stocked by the Virginia Department of Inland Fisheries and paid for by fishing licenses.

In 1994 a court case was convened to decide ownership. The landowners brought a float guide to court, contending that he had floated through their property with a fishing client without first obtaining permission. The final decision was to acknowledge the king's grants, and this has been upheld by the Virginia Supreme Court and will stand. This has had explosive implications for other streams along which numerous landowners possess antique crown grants. Fishermen who have floated and waded the James, Shenandoah, Rappahannock, and Potomac Rivers for generations could find themselves banned from those waters by private owners.

Fishing in the tailwater immediately beneath the dam is still fairly good. Below that 1000-yard stretch the stream has been largely privatized by landowners. It is a good idea to carefully observe the posted signs near the access points. You should also note that when floating through these private waters it is a misdemeanor to show fishing equipment.

Who's right and who's wrong? The landowners are of course within their legal rights to banish public fishing from their property. The Virginia Department of Game and Inland Fisheries is also right to stop stocking those private waters. But the end result is that much of Virginia's premier public trout stream, the Jackson River, has been largely taken away. Fortunately the regulated water upstream in Hidden Valley is still accessible and affords the best of Jackson River fly-fishing. Because this area is surrounded by public land, it is hoped that generations to come will be allowed to enjoy Hidden Valley.

JERRY'S RUN

Stream Type Freestone

Maps USGS Jerry's Run; DeLorme 52

Access From I-64 headed west from Covington, take the Jerry's Run Trail exit, almost to the West Virginia line. Turn left at the stop sign onto FR 198, which immediately becomes a single-lane, unpaved two-track. The road parallels Jerry's Run downstream, where it becomes FR 69. Where it diverges left up Brushy Mountain, there is a dirt lane leading right, with the usual understated ROUGH ROAD sign.

Jerry's Run is one of Virginia's highly visible streams that manages to retain its identity despite notoriety. The angler-athlete should be prepared to hike in to the most desirable native trout stretch, as the stream diverges right, away from the road. The only access from that point is a short, rutty road leading to a walking trail along the stream, which becomes very dim in spots but continues for around 4 miles. At the national forest boundary Jerry's Run flows into a fair-sized pond, which marks the end of trout fishing. There is no access from below, as below the pond the land belongs to the CSX Railroad, with emphatic NO TRESPASSING signs posted about.

There are enough feeder streams to maintain fishing through a dry September, and it's an ideal location for trying small autumn terrestrials. You will more than likely have the stream to yourself during this season. This may be due to both a lack of autumn stocking of Jerry's Run and the opening of bow-hunting season occupying outdoor sportsmen around the same time.

Jerry's Run is a slate-bottom stream with a gentle gradient throughout its length, with consequently only a few really deep holes. From the cut bank around 6 feet high you can look into the glass-clear shallows and spot a few decent-sized rainbows. Once located, these heavy-bodied fish can be stalked carefully from downstream. Apparently, there's a lack of aquatic insects, with an abundance of small minnows. Some surface feeding has been spotted, but its objectives were too small for recognition—probably gnats or similar small terrestrials.

The upstream stretch is 5 minutes away from the interstate exit bearing its name, so as might be expected, you won't immediately find the darting native trout shapes there that are apparent in the less convenient Appalachian streams. Farther downstream, where there is a 4-mile stretch with no vehicle access, the brook trout are more numerous in direct proportion to the lack of discarded beverage cans.

The surrounding national forest land has been timbered over within the last 15 years, so there are streamside clearings with enough backcasting room to place a fly from some distance away. This is a necessity because of the clarity of this shallow water, and because these are rod-wise fish that flee at the first sign of movement.

At one point there is a feeder stream flowing beneath the road and into a 10-foot-deep hole. There are signs of strenuous stream management here, with stones encased in woven wire and partial dams. The hole is probably heavily stocked, and just as heavily harvested by anglers who can step from their vehicles and cast into the pool. This is typical of the upper stretch, and fly-fishermen looking for natives should continue downstream until the path is less clearly trampled down.

A hatch of blue-winged olives makes this day's fishing even livelier than usual on the Laurel Fork in Highland County.

LAUREL FORK (HIGHLAND COUNTY)

Stream Type Freestone

Maps USGS Snowy Mountain, Thornwood; DeLorme 64, 65

Access Formerly, the most convenient access to Laurel Fork was from the east, down Christian Run Trail. That route is somewhat complicated by a locked gate on FR 457. It is recommended that you take US 250 west out of Monterey for approximately 20 miles. Then turn right on WVA 28 near Thornwood, West Virginia. Follow 28 for a little over 6.5 miles, where it intersects with FR 106. Turn right and follow FR 106. There are three possible trails leading south of the road to the stream—Locust Run Trail, Slab Camp Run Trail, and Bearwallow Run Trail. The first two of these take you farther downstream but necessitate walking 3.75 and 4 miles, respectively. The third, Bearwallow Run Trail, is only 2.75 miles long but has the disadvantage of taking you farther upstream. Still, you can begin fishing earlier, and you have less of a walk out later in the day. If you're headed for Bearwallow Run Trail, the most direct route is to take VA 642 to the right off WVA 28 at Thornwood. Then turn left onto FR 106 and go about 3.5 miles. This will bring you to Bearwallow from the south, with space to park beside

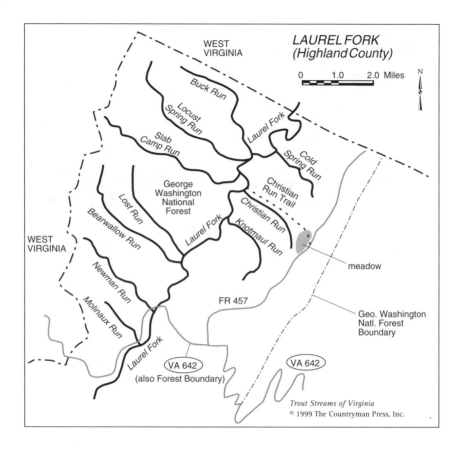

LAUREL FORK
(Highland County)

0   1.0   2.0 Miles   N

WEST
VIRGINIA

Buck Run

Locust
Spring Run

Slab
Camp Run

Laurel Fork

Cold
Spring Run

George
Washington
National
Forest

Christian
Run Trail

Lost Run

Christian Run

Bearwallow Run

Laurel Fork

Knotmaul Run

WEST
VIRGINIA

meadow

Newman Run

FR 457

Geo. Washington
Natl. Forest
Boundary

Molinaux Run

Laurel Fork

VA 642
(also Forest Boundary)

VA 642

Trout Streams of Virginia
© 1999 The Countryman Press, Inc.

the road. Just be sure to allow enough twilight for good visibility during the hour or more walk back to your vehicle.

All of these trails are well maintained, due to a moderate number of hikers, but may not always be clearly marked. The nearly 11,000 forest service acres can absorb the traffic, and the nearly 3-mile hike to the stream weeds out all but the most hardy fly-fishers.

One access to this stream is FR 457, following the crest of Middle Mountain. A four-wheel drive is desirable, as this is just a two-track through the trees for most of the way. There is now a locked gate, and the walk to Christian Run Trail is very time-consuming. When you park at the gate and walk through this grass, you realize it's wild native bluegrass, one clue to the uniqueness of this environment. At the far end of the meadow is a maple tree with two blue blazes, designating the trailhead. The walk, paralleling a small feeder stream, takes about 40 minutes, if you respect the leaf-covered stones that tend to tip underfoot. Christian Run Trail takes you to a strategic spot to begin fishing the Laurel Fork, right at about the lower third of the stream. You can walk downstream a fair distance and fish some deep holes back up, but upstream from the trail offers almost the same quality of fishing. For an adventure never to be forgotten, fish the 8 miles from the West Virginia border up to the VA(s) 642 bridge. Eight miles may not seem like much, but these will fill up your day with tough, rewarding native trout fishing.

The first look at Laurel Fork in early spring will take your breath away if you're accustomed to the small, high-mountain streams of Highland County. This is a big, boisterous, hard-charging waterway, with many holes over 6 feet deep, usually requiring chest waders for working most efficiently. Later, during the heat of summer, the water level may drop as much as 3 feet, causing the stream to shrink to much less than its usual 30- to 35-foot width. There are still brook trout to be had, but nothing to compare with the action during early-spring hatches.

In early morning when the sun just tops Middle Mountain, the rhododendron leaves silver up. There is an absence of footprints, and no sign of litter here, except for one Dr. Scholl's moleskin pad that I found, which some fisherman discarded after surrendering to his blisters.

This 10,000-acre tract of the George Washington National Forest remains just about as it was after the timber cutting died down early in this century. There are no utility poles, no houses, and not a sound except for a pileated woodpecker working a long way off. Most significantly, there are no roads downstream except for the barely drivable forest road. To reach the lower section of this 4,000-foot-elevation drainage, you must be prepared to walk.

As you make your first cast of the day, you can see rare red spruce on the far bank. Also here are northern hardwoods found nowhere else in the state. Although very rare now, you may catch a glimpse of a showshoe rabbit. Laurel Fork contains the largest concentration of threatened, endangered, and sensitive species in the entire George Washington National Forest. Bear sightings are frequent, and it's possible you may hear a cub whining in the woods. Another frequent inhabitant, unfortunately, is the timber rattler, and in midsummer you are all too likely to see one near the trail. There is a den that has existed next to the stream probably for centuries, and you may wish to delay your trip here until after hot weather, when the rattlers will have cooled down some.

On an April morning there may be no sign of a hatch, as this stream can be fairly cold in early spring. The ranks of 15- to 20-foot rhododendrons shield it from the sun until almost noon. But even this early in the year, the hatches can suddenly begin to swarm.

Author's Note *The first week in April 1994, at about 1 PM, I was surrounded by an explosion of* Ephemerella *on the Laurel Fork. In the morning there had been only a few midges, and I was taking* *mostly small brookies on black ants. But in early afternoon the hatches really started to swirl around me. First were march browns, followed by a burst of blue-winged quills, which became the killer fly of the day. There were also some quill gordons, a small species of stonefly, and a few big lumbering sulphurs. But the blue-wings were the most numerous and continued to hatch until almost 3 in the afternoon. That kind of satisfying mayfly activity is not typical on Virginia's mountain streams, if there really is any typical mayfly behavior.*

In mid-June I returned with a minister friend, Fred Webb, to the same section of the Laurel Fork. A 2-week drought had drastically changed the character of the stream and the quality of the fishing. The brook trout were smaller and there were fewer of them, leading to the conclusion that the larger fish may have migrated downstream to deeper water.

On that April day, when I first fished Laurel Fork, it was among the best native trout fishing I have experienced in Virginia. These were healthy, chunky, tail-walking brook trout, bright orange to the tips of their fins. I am told that 16-inchers are not uncommon here, although my catch averaged 8 to 10 inches. It is purely a brook trout stream, although down toward the West Virginia border I am told some sizable browns have wandered upstream into Virginia. I hooked and lost one of these during my day's fishing.

MAURY RIVER

Stream Type Freestone

Maps USGS Goshen; DeLorme 53

Access From I-81 take East Lexington exit 195 west on VA 39. Follow it to the Goshen Pass scenic area through which the Maury River flows.

On VA 39 between Goshen and I-81, the area called Goshen Pass is one of the most breathtaking bits of scenic beauty in Virginia. The Maury River is another roadside stream, but there's enough of it to accommodate a fair crowd of cruising anglers. It requires some patience to fish here, as it's likely to be dredged out by bait-fishermen shortly after stocking earlier in the season. But the Maury is one of those streams that might be worth a visit in June, when the proximity of good bass fishing nearby, indeed on the lower reaches of the Maury itself, may filter out some competition.

Higher up, at an area called Devil's Kitchen, there are stretches of class 3, 4, and 5 white-water canoeing, some of Virginia's best. As you might gather, it is advisable to wear chest waders here and to step forward with care in these rapids. Farther down, below the white water, there are some wide pools with plenty of cleared space for backcasting, an ideal location for sharpshooting at rising fish with Light Cahills or Hendricksons. Around dusk, or even just after, a large White Moth may coax some lure-wise brown from its favorite boulder.

MILL CREEK

Stream Type Limestone

Maps USGS Millboro; DeLorme 53, 65

Access From I-81 take the East Lexington exit 139 west on VA 39. Follow it through the town of Goshen, above which Mill Creek parallels 39.

Any trout enthusiast driving down VA 39 toward Goshen Pass will be distracted by the inviting stretch of Mill Creek paralleling the highway. This is a busy two-lane road, with little room to pull off onto the shoulder. Nevertheless, there is good trout water along VA 39 for several miles before the road reaches the town of Goshen. And even there, behind the Mill Creek Cafe, the water looks fishable.

Best results may be had along that portion of Mill Creek beginning at the Rockbridge–Bath county line, where moderately impressive boulders cause the water to pause and cascade down into deep holes. Like many active Virginia mountain streams, the Mill is conducive to fishing wet rather than dry. A dry fly has a hard time staying above water among the heavy riffles and falls. But as the prominent trout author E. R. Hewitt said back in the '30s, 80 percent of a trout's diet consists of underwater life-forms—30 percent nymphs plus others.

Woolly Worms do particularly well in the heavy water of Mill Creek when cast upstream into cascading water and allowed to run into the depths beneath. If that's not working, switching to Muddlers or other minnow-imitation streamers might stir up the trout population.

One of the burdens of fishing in Appalachia is parting the rhododendrons up some mountain draw and seeing four anglers, one at each corner of a choice pool. This will not happen on Mill Creek. It's a "drive-in" stream, and that is both a blessing and a curse. On the positive side, it may be cruised from VA 39 to spot the most inviting and least populated waters. On the negative side, as it is so public, it can have multiple vehicles parked above its choice pools, particularly on weekends early in the season. Later on, when the mayflies become thicker and the competition thins out, there's more elbow room on this stream, which incidentally has enough miles of fishing water to absorb a goodly number of bug-watchers.

MOSSY CREEK

Stream Type Limestone

Maps USGS Parnassus; DeLorme 66

Special Regulations Fishing restricted to single-hook artificial flies; creel limit one fish per day; all fish less than 20 inches long must be handled carefully and returned unharmed to the water; possession of fish less than 20 inches long on this water is illegal; possession of bait on this water is illegal; fishing permitted year-round; access must be at designated parking and fence-crossing points; wading, camping, and fires are prohibited. Written permission to fish is needed, as this water is private property; the landowner's rights must be respected, and failure to do so may result in loss of fishing privileges. Permission slips may be obtained at the Virginia Game and Inland Fisheries office in Verona.

Access Take the Weyer's Cave exit east off of I-81. Go north on US 11 and turn west onto VA(s) 646. Turn south onto VA 42 and proceed to VA(s) 613, which is a gravel road. Turn west on 613 and proceed to marked parking areas.

At the south shank of the Shenandoah Valley is the stream considered number one for trout by many informed Virginia fly-fishers. Certainly during late summer and early fall, when hoppers are falling into the stream, the Mossy's big browns will explode onto imitation cricket or grasshopper lures. Regardless of the unwinnable debate over which is first in Virginia's family of trout streams, Mossy Creek ranks high. And it makes an ideal first stop for anyone beginning their exploration of western Virginia's trout habitat. It's also a good test area for the neophyte fly-caster, as its gentle, riffled pools and grassy banks are free of the usual laurel or hemlock branches grabbing for unwary fly hooks.

Thanks to constant caretaking by Trout Unlimited, Mossy is a "tame" stream, carefully manicured, flowing through pastureland reminiscent of the famous limestone streams of central Pennsylvania with their whopping-big brown trout. Turnstiles make cattle fences easy to negotiate without damage to the landowners' strands. There are no cans or polystyrene boxes littering the banks, the immaculate appearance of the area speaking well of the careful fishermen-landowner relationship that exists here.

Mossy Creek originates at a large limestone spring in the old millpond at Mount Solon. The fishable section flows for a little over 7 miles through private grazing land, with access only at designated parking sites and fence crossings. At present only 3 miles are open to public fishing.

Despite its name, the streambed contains no true moss, but rather a proliferation of rooted aquatic plants. Fishing wet flies produces occasional

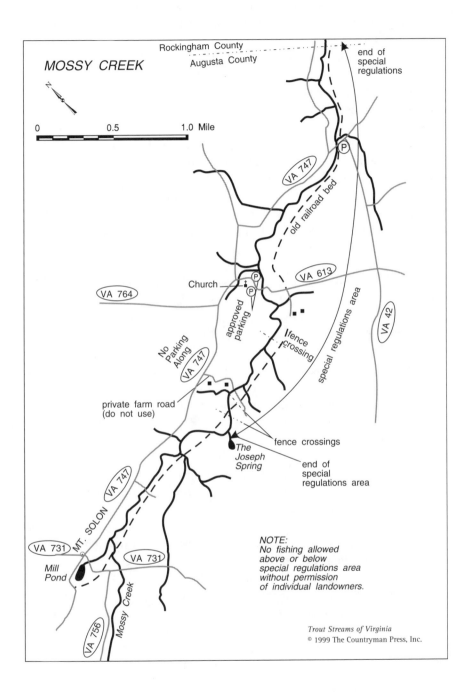

MOSSY CREEK

Rockingham County
Augusta County

end of
special
regulations

0   0.5   1.0 Mile

VA 747

old railroad bed

VA 613

Church

VA 764

approved parking

No Parking Along VA 747

fence crossing

special regulations area

VA 42

private farm road
(do not use)

fence crossings

The
Joseph
Spring

end of
special
regulations area

VA 747

MT. SOLON

VA 731

VA 731

Mill
Pond

VA 756

Mossy Creek

NOTE:
No fishing allowed
above or below
special regulations area
without permission
of individual landowners.

Trout Streams of Virginia
© 1999 The Countryman Press, Inc.

"hangs," which are easily freed up by snapping off a succulent watercress stem. Large springs feed in at frequent intervals, keeping the water at stable temperatures during the summer.

An active brown trout fingerling-stocking program was started on Mossy Creek in 1976 and is constantly under expansion. In 1989 electro-fishing of 72 browns produced two dozen fish between 12 and 16 inches, and six rod-benders greater than 16 inches in length. The Mossy also contains a few smallmouth and rock bass, but they have difficulty surviving the voracious big browns' appetites. Due to careful stream management, there is a sizable population of holdovers, supplemented by annual stockings of 5- to 6-inch fingerlings.

The stream averages 15 feet in width, with pools over 20 feet wide at most. Such close quarters makes for a little difficulty casting and working flies with a good drift. Delicate ties of standard dry patterns work best on the lure-wise trout in this stream's flat water.

During the prime hatching season, patterns for Mossy and most of Virginia's other trout waters can be covered by old standby dry flies such as Ginger Quill, Adams, Light Cahill, Trico, and Coachman patterns. During the gentle Virginia autumn and winter, terrestrial drys can be effective through most of the season, with year-round hatches. At the beginning of the hopper season a smaller, less obvious pattern such as a Letort number 16 is preferred. During the crisper months it is helpful to have a good supply of such terrestrials as black flying ants and the Crowe Beetle Dry.

Like the majority of Virginia's trout streams, the Mossy is open year-round. On a warm day in February, when the first bloodroot sprouts begin pushing through, this is a fine place to take out that primal spring urge to wet a fly. Despite a slight milky color of the water this time of year, some smaller trout are very receptive to wets such as weighted number 12 Muddlers and Pheasant Tail nymphs. A big black Woolly Bugger may tempt a larger brown to lash out of its winter sulk beneath the bank.

Make no mistake, Mossy Creek is not typical of Virginia's trout streams, which for the most part are boisterous mountain rapids with plunge pools formed by the boulders below. Nevertheless, it is a privilege to fish the manicured Mossy because of the obvious care that has been taken to keep this a prime trout fishery. For someone just entering the world of Virginia fly-fishing, this is an ideal location, with clear space for backcasts and an abundance of flat water furnishing predictable action throughout the year. A model of stream management, Mossy Creek affords a glimpse of the ideal, healthier future in store for Virginia's already flourishing trout program.

POTOMAC RIVER

Stream Type Limestone

Maps USGS Monterey; DeLorme 65

Access Follow US 220 north out of Monterey, the seat of Highland County. Pass the Virginia Trout Hatchery to the right and continue north to VA(s) 642, where a left turn puts you alongside the newborn Potomac.

This is not the Potomac of Washington Tidal Basin fame, but rather the headwaters of the big river. Here George Washington could have flipped a tuppence across the Potomac with no strain to his presidential thumb. A bureaucrat originally anchored in Highland County derived some satisfaction driving to downtown D.C. each morning, looking at the Potomac's broad expanse and remembering its humble spring-fed origin.

Turning left just before US 220 reaches the West Virginia border, you follow the Potomac upstream 4.6 miles, all of which is stocked with trout by the state. At first there is a short stretch running through woods, but above that the river is totally surrounded by livestock pasturage—sheep in one field, cattle in another. You may assume from that that the Potomac will never be classic trout water, and you're probably correct. But if you're fishing other streams in the area, such as the Jackson and Bullpasture Rivers or Back Creek, the Potomac is worth a side trip. After all, how many people can say they caught a trout from the Potomac? In fact, wild rainbows are prevalent in the upper half.

Because it's a meadow stream for the most part, a visit there will involve looking down from the road to a shining bronze ribbon cutting through green pasture. Then as one enters the village of Blue Grass on VA 642, a conspicuous sign by the road reads: CAUTION—NEW TRAFFIC PATTERN. This turns out to be Blue Grass's new, and only, stop sign, erected in the middle of town. Then the Potomac continues upstream through one livestock ranch after another. One wonders how the state stocking officials get through those hundreds of yards of grazing land to deposit their trout in the Potomac.

Just upstream from Blue Grass there is a dam and the vestige of a mill. The series of cascades descending below the dam offers some promise to the wet-fly caster. Even though the mill is in the village of Crab Bottom, the waters below it include some excellent trout habitat.

One could spend a day on the Potomac exploring the fishing possibilities, but also just enjoying the mountain meadow scenery, reminiscent of Switzerland. Occasional flights of goldfinches swoop across the stream, swift and brilliant against the green fields. The relatively gentle mountains rise slowly on either side, level enough to support the prosperous ranches. The mountaintops are a reminder that Highland County has the greatest average altitude of any county east of the Mississippi.

POUNDING MILL CREEK

Stream Type Freestone

Maps USGS Covington; DeLorme 52

Access From I-64 westbound take the US 220 cutoff, proceeding into the Covington city limits. Turn right on East Dolly Ann Drive, which is VA(s) 625, paved at first but rapidly becoming dirt and gravel where state maintenance ends. It then becomes FR 125, paralleling Pounding Mill Creek to the top of Fore Mountain.

The lower section of Pounding Mill Creek is posted by private landowners who have actually fenced it off. Where the pavement ends there is a sign indicating that FR 125 is a single-lane road with turnouts for passing. Here you come across the first sign nailed to a sycamore tree proclaiming TROUT-STOCKED WATERS. It is somewhat encouraging to note that the local service-station operators a few blocks away are unaware of how to reach Pounding Mill via Dolly Ann Drive. The road is worth finding, however, as the drive through to Clifton Forge is a rarely experienced flight across high mountaintops, with sheer drop-offs and roadsides shot through with the color of cardinal flowers, yellow-eyed Susans, and Dutchman's-breeches during the summer.

Pounding Mill Creek is a good stream to avoid during hot summer months, when it becomes little more than a rivulet, about as wide as one's forearm. Even with the spring rains, this is a small stream, really small, making the uninformed fly-fisher ask, "What am I doing here?" The answer lies in the many stocked and wild rainbows and wild brook trout scurrying for safety. For its size, this stream has a healthy and lively fish population— few if any of them citation sized, but many quite ready to try the patience of a camouflaged stalker throughout a morning. If you're not a connoisseur of small crystalline watercourses trickling through heavy rhododendrons, then avoid Pounding Mill.

It's a gravel-bed stream with sizable enough boulders to afford shelter for trout. There has been some streambed management here, with granite ripraps at the lower section. Various hurricanes have molded this section of the stream into islands and small dams that have probably improved the habitat. Farther upstream, where the hemlock overgrowth becomes heavier, there are nervous native trout darting away at alarming speed. Terrestrials are indicated here, with red and black ants recommended, along with hoppers during the summer.

Despite the lack of any water of appreciable depth upstream, there are logs placed across the stream by conservators, half-sawed in the center to form miniature waterfalls. From 20 yards away you can see a swarm of native brook trout beneath these falls, grateful for the oxygen bath during hot months.

Perhaps the most striking feature of Pounding Mill Creek is its testimony to a concentrated effort to save streams as small as this one. High up the mountain, where it becomes a shallow summertime trickle, there are still trout-stocking signs posted, along with one poster reading SAVE DEN TREES. FR 125 rides along the crest of Fore Mountain, in some places looking down a cliff to the tips of 100-foot chestnut oaks. Little traveled, except by a few timber trucks, this one-lane drive is a treat in itself, leading eventually to other fly-fishing opportunities along Smith Creek near Clifton Forge.

SMITH CREEK (ALLEGHANY COUNTY)

Stream Type Freestone

Maps USGS Clifton Forge; DeLorme 52

Access From I-81 take the US 220 exit north to Clifton Forge. Go through town to VA(s) 606, which proceeds north of Clifton Forge to Smith Creek, which is regulated from the town to the water-treatment plant. Above the reservoir is a walk-in stretch.

Unlike most small mountain streams, Smith Creek has enough flow to allow fishing even during the low-water months. The upper section contains a series of natural stone sluiceways entrapping pools of water 4 or 5 feet deep. Because of the glassy clarity of these sluices, fish can spot even the slightest careless move, but a camouflaged, cautious stalk from downstream can bring you within casting distance. Terrestrials are the main food supply here, as the creek has few mayfly hatches on its swift surface.

What impresses one most about Smith Creek is the multitude of brook trout shapes darting upstream in nearly every pool. These are both natives and holdovers, with brook trout only being stocked here. The upper section flows through deep woods, where the aroma of aging damp leaves overcomes the occasional unpleasant wafting from Covington's paper mill, some miles to the southwest. Although closely paralleled by VA 606, this colorful stream shows little sign of fishing pressure. It displays one classic small waterfall and plunge pool after another. This frequency of irresistible fishing spots may explain the good holdover and native population, dispersing pressure throughout the entire length of the Smith. Another asset of this stream is the regulated stretch downstream, which may be the best fishing of all—certainly when it comes to brown trout.

Despite the time of day, the weather, or pressure of scheduling, there is no choice but to fish these bubbling emerald pools. There is simply no alternative. It is surprising to find small, voracious brookies in each pool in sufficient quantity to keep one fishing for over an hour without rehooking one. With the enthusiasm and appetite of the young of any species, these vibrant little trout clear the water after a Letort Hopper when it's lifted from the surface. What's even more encouraging is to see the larger brethren of these small members of the congregation at the last moment turn away from the temptation of a wet-fly hackle. Such action can be had at midday even during the heat of August, when the coolness on one's bare shins provides refreshing relief.

These are all lively, healthy fish, with plenty of dace, small crayfish, gray spiders, and moths providing nourishment. There is an abundance of these and other insects in the crevices of the purple shale lining the banks. One caution, however, concerns the tendency of the thin stone to present a seemingly sturdy foothold only to crumble like cake frosting when stepped on. Without careful choice of steps, this could lead to a tumble down the steep bank into a sudden, breath-robbing bath—fine in August, perhaps, but a little too startling in April.

SPRING RUN

Stream Type Limestone

Maps USGS Williamsville; DeLorme 65

Access Spring Run may be reached via VA(s) 678, which turns east off VA 39 just north of Millboro Springs. Follow 678 for 14.5 miles, almost to Williamsville, and turn right at the COURSEY SPRINGS FISH CULTURAL STATION sign. For those planning to fish Bath and Highland Counties, Spring Run is a good starting point for determining which mayfly hatches are on the streams or which terrestrials are being taken.

The outstanding feature of Spring Run is that it is the outflow of the state trout hatchery at Coursey Springs. The stream is not a part of the hatchery but is stocked regularly from it. One might be tempted to think fishing Spring Run is like dropping a fly into one of the hatchery holding ponds. Nothing could be farther from the truth.

These are wary fish, looking up at you from the diamond-clear water, ready to scamper into the aquatic weeds at the slightest movement. It is recommended that you stalk these rainbows just as you would wild trout. And if you see the faint outlines of fish finning calmly in the current, chances are they have seen you first and have not the slightest inclination to take your fly. A much more productive strategy is to cast upstream next to beds of cress, which with luck will screen you from sight.

The distance from the hatchery dam downstream to where Spring Run empties into the Cowpasture River is around 900 yards. It is no hardship to walk a careful distance away from the stream down to the confluence and then fish back upstream. Where the creek empties into the Cowpasture there is some deep water, and sizable trout may be hiding away from the fishing traffic. But don't be surprised at hooking into a 2-foot fallfish, which may give you a "brown trout" fight for a brief period before tiring.

This is purely a meadow stream, flowing quietly down a slight gradient, with long stretches of quiet but relatively shallow water between. Terrestrials are sometimes the preferred lures, particularly when hoppers are observed in the streamside fields. Spring Run rainbows sometimes strike at your leader knot, which some theorize indicates a preference for gnats. Smaller flies do appear to be more successful than large, and casting is simplified by lack of bushes to hang up backcasts.

A bonus of stalking Spring Run trout is the opportunity to observe their hatchery brethren and see what they are siphoning off the surface of Coursey Springs. Occasionally an osprey will remove a link from the food chain, carrying off a small rainbow from a holding pond for its breakfast. The hatchery opens at 8 AM, along with fishing privileges at Spring Run. Fishing stops at 3 PM, and the hatchery road is chained shut to visitors at 3:30.

4 | James River Drainage Area

As you turn east off I-81 onto I-64 toward Charlottesville, the terrain is gentle and rolling, with mostly farmland in sight. The highway begins a sudden climb up Afton Mountain, and at Rockfish Gap you are suddenly on top of the Blue Ridge, where Skyline Drive and the Blue Ridge Parkway join. For the trout angler this is decision time. You can elect to turn north and explore some of the 30 native trout streams within the Shenandoah National Park boundaries, or you can turn south and follow the Blue Ridge Parkway toward the Montebello Fish Cultural Station and the St. Mary's Wilderness Area with its river of the same name.

At Irish Gap on the parkway, you can turn east and discover the upper Piney River, especially welcome on a warm day, when you can fish beneath the cooling caverns of hemlock. The Pedlar River watershed, leading down to the Lynchburg Reservoir, offers not only the Pedlar, but also Little Irish Creek and enough other small streams to fill a day.

The streams in this area are relatively sedate, leading down to pastureland and small villages, unlike the area west of I-81 where the mountains dominate. In fact, some of the top fly-fishing in the James River Drainage is found in the suburbs of Waynesboro, where a regulated stretch of the South River meanders between clipped suburban lawns.

BUFFALO RIVER (AMHERST COUNTY)

Stream Type Freestone

Maps USGS Forks of Buffalo; DeLorme 54

Special Regulations On the North Fork of the Buffalo and its tributaries within the George Washington National Forest, fishing is restricted to single-hook artificial lures; creel limit six fish per day; all fish less than 9 inches long must immediately be returned unharmed to the water; possession of

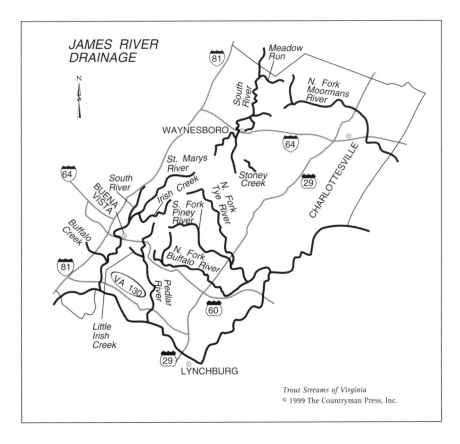

JAMES RIVER DRAINAGE

Trout Streams of Virginia
© 1999 The Countryman Press, Inc.

fish less than 9 inches long is illegal; possession of bait on this water is illegal. All portions of the Buffalo described here are within the George Washington National Forest.

Access From I-81, take US 60 east through Buena Vista to Forks of Buffalo, where VA(s) 635 turns north. Follow 635 to the end, where the road becomes little more than a trail into the George Washington National Forest.

The Buffalo River's North Fork is sometimes more accurately labeled Buffalo Creek, being one of the Blue Ridge watershed's typical moderate-to high-gradient smaller streams. It is not to be confused with the special-regulations stretch of another Buffalo Creek, in Rockbridge County.

Be prepared to make a day of it on the Buffalo, beginning with some slow grinding of your four-wheel-drive gears up the random boulder roadbed at the end of VA(s) 635. At some point your spinal column and truck springs reach a point of no return. But the wear and tear on tires is more than compensated by the ravenous wild trout population of this stream, many of them in the 8- to 10-inch category.

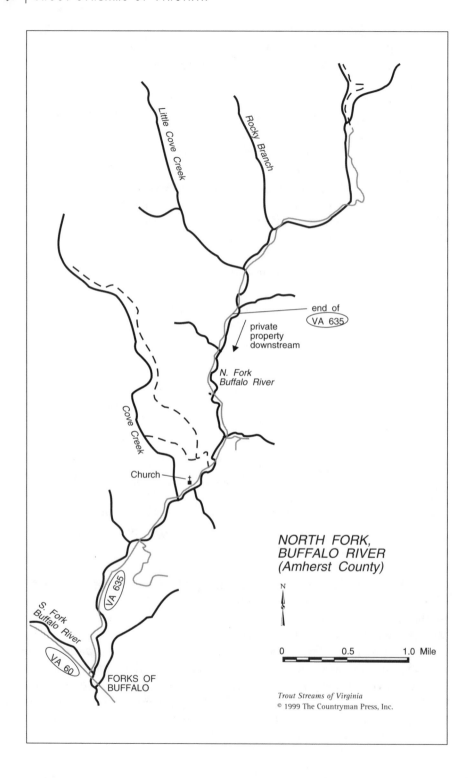

Little Cove Creek

Rocky Branch

end of
VA 635

private
property
downstream

N. Fork
Buffalo River

Cove Creek

Church

**NORTH FORK,
BUFFALO RIVER
(Amherst County)**

N

0   0.5   1.0 Mile

VA 635

S. Fork
Buffalo River

VA 60

FORKS OF
BUFFALO

Trout Streams of Virginia
© 1999 The Countryman Press, Inc.

Author's Note *My first experience with the Buffalo was in mid-March, a couple of weeks after the season's opening. There was not another soul around, and very little debris from opening-day activities. Forty-five minutes of casting a series of wet minnow imitations produced only one small brookie and a twisted left ankle. Sitting beside a plunge pool, nursing sprained ligaments, I noticed a march brown hovering over the water. Tying on a fly of the same name, I cast from a seated position, immediately hooking a 7-inch trout. That small pool yielded four more brookies, none of them going the required 9 inches, but all surprisingly strong for their size.*

Moving downstream, where I had previously been skunked, I picked up some 8- to 10-inch fish where small tributaries fed in. As usual these more mature trout were warier, and in many cases looked my March Brown over carefully only to give it a tail slap. This one fly landed over two dozen fish before it was frazzled beyond deception.

This is not a wading stream; rather, be prepared for some rock climbing along the banks. Many of the boulders along the way are more than 10 feet in height, and these towering slabs shape the character of the Buffalo, forming the most perfect plunge pools in this area of the Blue Ridge. Within almost every pool is a lively population of brook trout, constantly on the move because of the short supply of minnows. In some cases giant rocks rest at the water's edge, bordered by narrow strips of sand and gravel. One way to use these is to cast around the corner of a boulder onto unseen stretches of clear water. This gets tricky, as the only indication of a dry-fly strike is the slight upstream tightening of line or sound of a splash.

Another technique is to climb atop a stone slab and edge your way carefully—very carefully—over a pool. From this high perch you can cast upstream onto clear and relatively shallow water without being spotted. The terrain and gradient of the Buffalo are reminiscent of a number of the Shenandoah National Park's wild trout streams. Only here in this remote corner of the George Washington National Forest, there is a better chance of finding yourself all alone on the stream.

IRISH CREEK

Stream Type Freestone

Maps USGS Cornwall, Montebello; DeLorme 54

Access Take I-81 to exit 195. Turn north onto US 11 past the Maple Hall Country Inn and go to the Sam Houston Wayside where a sign indicates VA(s) 785 leading to VA(s) 716. Take 716, go left on 706, right on 710, and come out at the Concord Church of the Brethren. Turn right on VA(s) 608 paralleling the South River downstream to where it joins Irish Creek. Turn left here on VA(s) 603 and drive up South Mountain, fishing as many alluring holes and rapids as you can fit into the day.

There are frequent gravel turnoffs above the stream as VA(s) 603 climbs South Mountain, most of them overlooking stunning visual treats, with white pines marching to the stream, whose banks are heavily bordered with wildflowers. At first glance the Irish, not to be confused with the Little Irish, appears to be the ideal of every mountain-stream connoisseur. And for the most part it is. But there are some ugly contrasts, such as a rusty old refrigerator with its feet sticking out of what otherwise would be some eminently fishable tailwater. This is an infrequent sight, and throughout the George Washington National Forest property the rangers patrol conscientiously. But there are some stretches of private land, and as sad testimony to the human condition, old tires and assorted other bits of rubbish have been pushed over the bank into heartbreakingly beautiful trout water. The desecration is brief, so pass through this put-and-take area up to where South Mountain's real treasures lie.

The water is crystalline, so trout may be spotted easily, even to the point that one can see what they are feeding on—quick, swirling movements after minnows, tail-up searching after nymphs along the bottom. Mayflies predominate, mostly march browns and hendricksons. The problem is finding a pool quiet enough to reveal the surface feeders.

Mother Nature has provided frequent rockslides, forming sluices through which the Irish rushes at a decent depth. At convenient points, the National Forest Authority has constructed walls from the abundant riverjacks (smooth stones) enclosed in wire mesh, protecting the stream's banks. As the road becomes steep, there are three levels of rock walls forming a backdrop for the Irish's thumbnail Niagara. Here is a treat for the eye, plus a 20-foot-deep basin of swirling water below containing trout large enough to break a 4-pound leader without showing themselves. This is fruitful territory for a larger nymph or streamer, such as a hair wing or Woolly Bugger.

Because of the water's clarity, you may be sure that the downstream fish will spot you as soon as your head pops up over a stone wall. Fishing upstream helps, as does visiting the Irish after a spring rain has turned it milky.

Overlooking the Irish during a lunch break, you'd think it impossible that anyone should ever tire of these emerald and crystal mountain gems. Their fragility is also apparent, however, as is the need for gentle treatment of the trout and their habitat. Fly-fishing here is an exercise in intricacy, with little opportunity to lash out with 30-foot casts as on the big waters, such as Virginia's Jackson River.

Far upstream the Irish begins to lose its boisterous identity and comes to look like any number of other small Appalachian Mountain gems, if you discount the occasional mallard drake floating about irritably. In early spring there probably would be a hen on the nest somewhere nearby. Here you will find wild trout.

Two notes of caution: Copperheads have been spotted among the fissures of the endless boulder piles that contain the Irish. So take your eye off the fly occasionally when taking a step. Second, the gravelly foothold on rock shelves 50 feet above the stream requires some concentration. As with many smaller trout waters, wading seldom if ever becomes necessary on the Irish. If one chooses to enter the water, rock ledges are usually covered with gritty sand or gravel, making for easy footing.

Shell and claw leavings from a raccoon's supper may indicate tying on a crayfish imitation. High up on the Irish's headwaters, however, the smaller native fish will have trouble swallowing a larger lure, so you may get strikes without hooking the fish. The abundance of crayfish may explain why your perfectly presented black gnat is being ignored by the trout. High on the Irish you are in hemlock country, and the dimly filtered light even at midday encourages moths to fly over the stream, making your White Moth fair game.

Driving up VA(s) 603, one begins to wonder if the abundance of tempting fishing waters will ever end, with the mountain-spring branches continually falling down into the creek. Where they empty in, there is a proliferation of underwater life-forms, not only crayfish but also mayfly and stonefly nymphs and small black snails. A dry-fly angler may be temporarily thwarted on the Irish. But there's no reason not to switch to a Pheasant Wing nymph or Green Beetle.

The luck of the Irish is that it has one picture-perfect little trout glen after another. The higher up South Mountain you go, the better chance of encountering wily little native brook trout.

LITTLE IRISH CREEK

Stream Type Freestone

Maps USGS Buena Vista; DeLorme 54

Access Little Irish Creek is an interesting contrast to the Pedlar River, and both streams are close enough to one another to be easily fished in a day. About 6 miles east of Buena Vista on US 60, turn south on FR 39. Follow FR 39 down the Pedlar nearly to the southern end of the Lynchburg Reservoir and turn west on FR 311. This one-lane gravel road parallels the Little Irish for several miles, and likely holes may be scouted from the road with ease.

Amid a maze of dirt and gravel roads east of the Pedlar River is a stream that is a delight to the eyes. The Little Irish stair-steps down to the

Pedlar in a series of cameo cascades. Each of these waterfalls has worn a hole in the granite 10 or 15 feet deep, and within these are trout to be had. The idea is to approach cautiously and let the natural downward current carry your nymph to the bottom. Brookies of surprising size can be caught in these waterfall lees. Between casts in the spring you can admire the pink trillium growing on the banks.

As you follow the Little Irish upstream, the stair steps become less dramatic, and instead of waterfalls you find short stretches of riffles ending in 5-foot-deep potholes. Each of these is a different challenge, to be studied from a distance and then approached taking maximum advantage of cover. This is not big water by any means. But a shiny-bodied number 20 black ant eased over partly submerged logs can make your day on the Little Irish.

MEADOW RUN (POTOMAC RIVER DRAINAGE)

Stream Type Freestone

Maps USGS Crimora; DeLorme 67

Access From within the Shenandoah National Park, drive to Skyline Drive milepost 92 and park there in the Wildcat Ridge parking area. Then follow the Wildcat Ridge Trail down 2.7 miles where it intersects with the Riprap Trail. The Riprap Trail follows Meadow Run downstream to the left and upstream if you turn right.

These Shenandoah streams are at their best within the park boundaries, where their hike-in access from the Skyline Drive preserves their solitude and fishing quality.

This small park stream runs very low during the summer yet maintains a surprising population of brook trout. Despite a scarcity of hatches there is a moderate amount of surface feeding on a variety of terrestrials.

For those who prefer solitude with their fishing, Meadow Run has plenty. Access to the stream requires over 3 miles of hiking, most of it on a smooth but steep trail well maintained by the Shenandoah National Park Service. Allow enough time to climb the Shenandoah Range back out before dark and wear strong hiking shoes or boots. Also, be at somewhat better than "couch potato" fitness. Waders are not a must but will be a slight convenience when the stream is running at capacity.

No hunting is permitted, so game proliferates along the trail. It is impossible not to encounter small animals, turkey, deer, and an occasional bear. There are signs posted in the park warning THIS IS BEAR COUNTRY, so don't be surprised to run across a bruin while you're fishing. These are park bears, accustomed to hikers, but possessing the same muscle, teeth, and claws as wild bears anywhere. So some judgment is required when encountering the rare bear—usually a mother with cubs—that does not immediately flee from a human.

> **Author's Note** *In mid-September of 1990, I was fishing the upstream section of Meadow Run when a slight rustle caused me to look up. Twenty-five yards downstream was a 200-pound female black bear and her two cubs. Scenting me, she stopped and took a hard look in my direction, while the cubs peeked around her knickers. Then she started toward me in a determined fashion. Armed only with a walking stick and a 7-foot Shakespeare WondeRod, I selected one of the few uninviting options open to me. Crouching toward her, I struck the stones in the trail with my staff and shouted at the top of my lungs. This frightened the cubs, which laid back their ears and ran. She turned toward them, then back toward me, and after a moment of consideration decided to follow the cubs. The thunder of her feet striking the ground is a sound I will never forget, and I will forever be grateful that the sound was fading rather than approaching.*

As with any jump-across mountain stream, the following rules apply on Meadow Run: Go slow; stay low; blend in (camouflage clothing works best, but at the very least wear "earth colors" that blend in with the background); stay thin (referring to leaders, of course: Despite the tendency of 6X to kink and become invisible, the results are worth the aggravation).

Along the lower stretch of Meadow Run to the Shenandoah National Park boundary, the brooks are smaller. Nudging the submerged roots of a downed tree can produce a family of 18 or 20 trout ranging from 9 inches down to "pinkie" fingerling size. They appear instantly and hang immobile like so many aquarium fish, gazing curiously at anglers who at that point can kiss any chance of catching them goodbye.

Paradoxically, farther upstream the fish are larger, although not as numerous. This may be due to the steeper gradient up the mountainside, which produces deeper holes beneath the cascades. Hatches are practically nonexistent, although they're more likely to occur down on the valley floor than up in bear country. Small terrestrials, even number 22 Jassids, are preferred. Meadow Run brook trout are terrestrial feeders, and lures should approximate ants, beetles, spiders, and small moths.

MOORMANS RIVER, NORTH FORK (POTOMAC RIVER DRAINAGE)

Stream Type Freestone

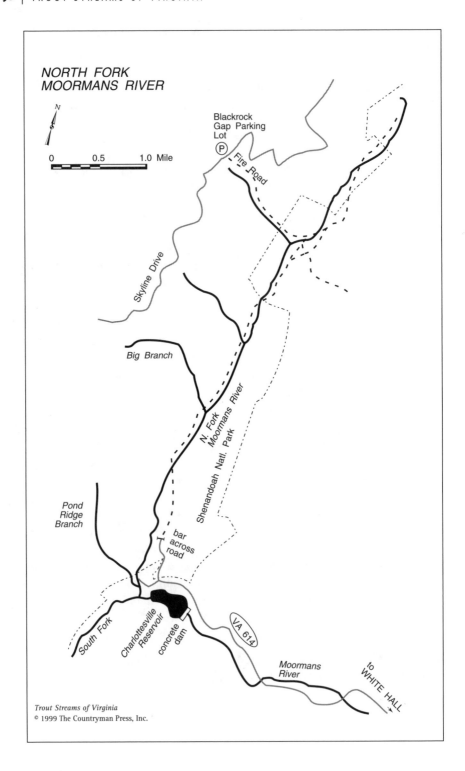

NORTH FORK
MOORMANS RIVER

N

0   0.5   1.0 Mile

Blackrock
Gap Parking
Lot
Ⓟ

Fire Road

Skyline Drive

Big Branch

N. Fork Moormans River

Shenandoah Natl. Park

Pond
Ridge
Branch

bar
across
road

South Fork

Charlottesville Reservoir

concrete dam

VA 614

Moormans
River

to
WHITE HALL

Trout Streams of Virginia
© 1999 The Countryman Press, Inc.

Maps USGS Brown's Cove; DeLorme 67

Special Regulations From the Shenandoah National Park boundary, this is catch-and-release water: fishing is restricted to artificial flies with single, barbless hooks; all fish must be handled carefully and returned immediately to the water; possession of fish, at any time, is illegal.

Access From I-64 east toward Charlottesville, take the exit at US 250 and follow it east to Yancey Mills and Sassy Lotus. From there take VA 240 to VA(s) 810 north. Follow 810 to the intersection with VA(s) 614 at White Hall. Turn left on 614, also known as Sugar Hollow Road. From a fairly good two-lane pavement, 614 becomes a 15 mph dirt road leading to the Charlottesville Reservoir, formed by damming the Moormans River.

To reach the stream from above, inside the Shenandoah National Park, go to the Blackrock Gap parking area at milepost 87 of the Skyline Drive. Cross the highway and walk down the North Fork Moorman's River Road. Eventually you'll pass through some private grazing land where hiking and fishing are permitted.

One is struck by the imposing concrete dam across the lower Moormans River, high enough to contain the water supply for the city of Charlottesville. Here there is no hunting, trapping, swimming, or camping, and fires are prohibited. But there is fishing, and the few people you meet are probably trout-fishing purists. The restrictions have led to an abundance of game, and it should be no surprise to see a fawn in early September, wearing summer red and spots, easing down the road toward you. Without fear of people, the deer approach close enough to imitate dogs getting ready to sniff your trouser leg.

The small feeder roads like VA(s) 614, around the periphery of the Shenandoah National Park, afford perhaps the best look at the trout potential. Shenandoah is said to have the heaviest traffic of our national parks, perhaps because of its proximity to eastern population centers. Even during the height of the vacation season, however, one may approach the Moormans from the lower boundary through the seldom-seen countryside in comparative solitude. Along the streams there may be a few anglers, but mainly you see Appalachian Trail hikers and other environmentally sensitive visitors.

At the tail of the reservoir you will see the first state trout-stocking signs. Above the dam, the North Fork of the Moormans becomes a typical Shenandoah drainage stream, very low and clear during the hot months. Fishing is possible but demanding at low water, and early spring is the right time to experience the Moormans. Even when the water is low, however, this stream is cold enough to support a lively trout population, including some

Just after this photo was taken, the angler released a nice rainbow back into its freestone pool.

nice browns. The stream is still recovering from extensive flood damage to the lower half in 1996.

The road upstream becomes a series of ditches with thin plateaus between, making a four-wheel drive vehicle desirable. After a couple of miles there is a bar blocking vehicle travel, with a sign indicating that all-terrain vehicles and trail bikes are prohibited. The message reads further that the Moormans is a catch-and-release stream from this point on. As might be expected, more and larger trout are spotted in the catch-and-release section. The sight of a trout finning in the pool 50 feet below you normally means that you might as well forget it; he has seen you as well. It is advisable to retreat slowly and approach the pool again from behind cover, even if that means casting blind over a boulder. These are wary fish, particularly during low water.

Turning over stones usually fails to produce any nymphs or stonefly larvae in the downstream section, but there is an abundance of shiners, crayfish, snails, and terrestrial insects. Farther upstream there is some surface feeding, and the food, cover, and pool depths are generally better near the top. An ideal way to see the Moormans is to park two vehicles, one above the dam and the other at Blackrock Gap, then fish upstream to the Skyline Drive.

PEDLAR RIVER

Stream Type Freestone

Maps USGS Buena Vista; DeLorme 54

Access Take US 60 for about 6 miles east from Buena Vista, then turn north on VA(s) 605. At national forest stop sign number 76, turn left to a rest area on the stream bank. Continuing farther on VA(s) 605 brings you to private land where stream access is prohibited. You can also take FR 39, a gravel road that follows the Pedlar downstream to the Lynchburg Reservoir.

Fishing the Pedlar takes you through an exhibit of the variety of trout angling in Virginia. As you move upstream, totally different habitats are successively revealed, reminding you of other spots on other streams. The bottom is gravel and small stones, providing good footing throughout the streambed.

There are constant reminders that a large beaver colony is lurking somewhere in the woods nearby. Sizable trees are felled, leaving the characteristic pointed stumps cut by beaver incisors. An occasional twig dam spans the Pedlar, behind which the stream has silted up, making for less-than-ideal trout habitat—unlike the effect of beaver dams on other streams.

At the George Washington National Forest Wayside, the Pedlar is barely wide enough to deserve the label *river*. But this stretch contains some deep holes, and from the many boot tracks appears to be heavily fished early in the season when brook and rainbow trout are stocked. Fishing upstream to a steel bridge, you'll observe a sharp change in the Pedlar's character. The stream narrows, holes are shallower, there is an abundance of rapids, and the streamside paths are less worn.

At the Oronoco equipment shelter, upstream within sight of the bridge, there is a dirt lane that dead-ends quickly. From there it is a short walk to a Pedlar somewhat different from the wider area downstream. It reverts to a mountain-spring creek here, calling for an assortment of small nymphs and wet flies. There is an abundance of small minnows in the backwaters, and minnow imitations such as a small sinking Muddler can be effective.

Following FR 39 downstream takes you to some steep and relatively remote terrain where there is a good holdover brown population. Fingerling browns are stocked in the upstream section, which remains mostly put-and-take.

PINEY RIVER, SOUTH FORK

Stream Type Freestone

Maps USGS Massies Mill; DeLorme 54

Access Turn off the Blue Ridge Parkway near Buena Vista onto US 60 and follow it east for approximately 4.4 miles. At Oronoco take a left on VA(s) 634 and go to Alto, continuing on VA(s) 634 until it becomes FR 63 at the point where public access begins within the George Washington National Forest. FR 63 parallels the South Fork of the Piney for a considerable distance.

Driving in from the lower reaches of the Piney River may tend to be a discouraging experience. The stream is jealously posted, with NO FISHING being the dominant theme, although someone is obviously doing a thorough job of private trout management with weirs and channel deflectors. Farther upstream on VA(s) 827 the water emerges from the George Washington National Forest, and there is public access plus stocking.

There are long, quiet stretches of Piney River just inside the national forest, where surface feeding may be observed. For the most part, though, this stretch is a rocky spillway through the mountains, with stair-step cascades and pools. Still, this is a put-and-take stretch.

For solitude of the most sublime nature, the country around the upper headwaters of this stream is the place to be, particularly during the hot months. A mature forest bends over the cascades, completing the coolness. For some reason this section of the Piney River shows little sign of wear. There is not a speck of trash, and the paths do not show any recent wading-boot tracks. Is it just possible that this is one of those streams that come close to deserving the label *untouched*? True, there is no truly untouched public trout stream in the eastern United States, but in this part of Virginia the Piney comes close. It is heartening to find a trout fishery of this quality so close to population and so relatively untainted by the detritus of civilization.

In some cases the whopping size of trout that make a pass at your

Hare's Ear Nymph can be startling. These are veterans of many seasons, so they don't always fall for even the best Coachman or nymph.

Unless you have plenty of time, don't bother to trek into the upper Piney. At every turn in the road there is another irresistible pool below that cries out to be fished. Typically there are great panlike expanses of granite that have deep basins carved into them by the millennia of cascading water. Below the boulders, in the foaming green turbulence, are some of the most gorgeously colored native brook trout anywhere in this state. Occasional pods of smaller natives show no reluctance in taking whatever is offered, although a wet Olive Dun may prove most consistent.

Showing up as jet black shapes beneath the surface, when taken from the water these 8-inch gems literally glow with purple-red spots and gold flecks equaled only by high-grade ore, the colors of nature found only in springwater native brookies. Even the most hardened game hog would have difficulty killing one of these specimens.

SOUTH RIVER

Stream Type Freestone

Maps USGS Cornwall; DeLorme 54

Access Take exit 195 from I-81, just north of Lexington. Follow US 11 north to the Sam Houston Wayside, turn right on VA(s) 785, which leads to 716. Go left on VA(s) 706 to 710, which leads past the Concord Church to the first public access. Turn right on 608 and follow the river downstream. This is an entirely different South River from the one running through Waynesboro, sometimes leading to confusion.

The paved road alongside South River makes this stream almost feasible to cast over from the bed of a pickup truck. It is accessible, and fishing pressure is heavy. This far upstream it doesn't really deserve to be called a river and is more an overgrown spring creek. It's hardly even 50 feet across. Some concrete low-water bridges, mostly washed away, provide good trout cover, though, so it's a worthwhile stream. One suggestion: Because of the stream's manicured banks and easy accessibility from a busy road, uncrowded areas are at a premium. You may improve your chances by making a wide circle downstream and fishing the tailwater upstream.

Around the village of Midvale, the gradient is steeper and the pools are deeper. Downstream is stocked heavily, and it might be assumed that the bait-fishers have been here. But wait—below a bridge is a tempting bit of tailwater that has been scanned by truckloads of fishermen. One can imagine the same conversation being repeated over and over: "Naw. Don't stop here. Everybody fishes at the bridge. It's bound to be fished out. Let's go down to where Irish Creek empties in." And yet this highly visible pool contains at least one tackle-busting brookie that attacks a weighted number 18 Muddler Minnow as if it were a sworn enemy. But that's what makes the South River worth trying: the frequency of rapids with good green holes beneath them, passed up by fishermen headed for the more rugged Irish Creek up the mountainside. Where the two streams meet in the flatlands there is a sufficient flow of water to deserve the name *river,* perhaps not in Idaho, but certainly in western Virginia.

Just south of Waynesboro, another South River runs through a residential area, where it maintains its identity as a trout fishery. There is a fishable-sized stocking here, with a delayed harvest. The stream is open for fishing October 1 and closes May 15. Some consider this unlikely area to be one of the best fly-fishing spots in the state.

STONEY CREEK

Stream Type Freestone

Maps USGS Waynesboro East; DeLorme 55

Access From parkway mile marker number 13 at Reed's Gap take VA(s) 664 east. Approximately 1 mile down the mountain is the Wintergreen gatehouse, where you can get directions to the Outdoor Center, where you obtain fishing passes. Or you can continue on down 664 for 6.5 miles until it dead-ends into VA 151. Turn left and proceed another 3.5 miles to a sign indicating the STONEY CREEK ENTRANCE. Turn left there and go to the administrative office, where passes are also available.

This particular Stoney Creek is one of several in Virginia. Despite being a privately owned stream, it deserves attention because of some unique features. Only 10 miles northeast of the acid-laden St. Mary's River, the Stoney has maintained a normal pH level. It may receive much the same acid deposition as the St. Mary's, but Stoney Creek's bedrock is a basalt called greenstone, which has potent acid-neutralizing properties, making it more resistant to acidification. It is fortunate in not sharing the sensitivity of many Shenandoah Park streams to the north.

The best way to fish Stoney Creek is by starting at the metal footbridge just above the power plant and working upstream. The going is strenuous, and most will find Shamokin Falls to be a good cutoff point for a day's fishing. Along the way are many little feeder streams, which are sired by a series of mountain springs, stair-stepping down from about 3,200 feet up, beginning at an area called Shamokin Springs.

It is this constant flow that keeps the stream temperature in the low 60s, even in July and August. In addition to brook trout, there are some browns

A check of the aquatic-insect population gives promise of good nymph fishing on Stoney Creek.

in the larger pools. There are also a few holdover rainbows, but they are no longer stocked. Virginia law states that if a species is no longer reproducing in a given stream, it will not be stocked there, and such was the case with rainbows here. Stocking is privately sponsored and takes place in March and usually also in the latter part of May. The resulting population usually flourishes until September.

Stoney Creek is relatively small, in spite of holding a good flow in summer. Most trout-feeding stations are in potholes near the bank or tiny plunge pools. It is somewhat of a shock to come across a sizable flat pool a few hundred yards below Shamokin Falls with plenty of room for casting. On the uphill bank there is a complex of old stone walls erected by settlers who lived in that hollow during the last century. On the right bank is the vestige of the Old Diamond Square Cemetery, where they buried their dead. It contains markers for many Confederate soldiers, most of whom died of smallpox during the Civil War.

Here you encounter a trail marked by blue blazes that is part of the Wintergreen Trail Hiking System, maintained by the Wintergreen Resort. You can follow it upstream to Shamokin or return to the power-plant footbridge where you started.

Along the banks there is evidence of volunteer work by the Flyfishers of Virginia, Trout Unlimited, and employees of Wintergreen. Each year the stream is selectively pruned: Branches are cut where overgrowth interferes with casting, but limbs overhead are left intact.

Caddis flies are a predominant hatch along the Stoney. As a Wintergreen executive put it, "Just about the time the sun goes down in July and August there is frequently a major caddis hatch. It's as though someone flips on a bug switch at five o'clock, when the sun starts to drop over that western ridge." There is also a good hatch of little yellow stoneflies, and either a size 14 stonefly tie or a stonefly nymph works pretty well then. In early spring there is a strong blue-winged olive hatch, which recurs periodically throughout the winter. Even if there is no surface activity apparent, nymphs can be very effective when you spot just a few blue-winged olives flying.

Stoney Creek is owned by the Wintergreen Community, and Wintergreen property owners may fish it free of charge. Day visitors may obtain a 1-day pass at either the Outdoor Center up on the mountain or Lake Monocan down in the Stoney Creek Recreation Facility. For Trout Unlimited or Virginia Flyfishers members, the cost is $10 per day; for nonmembers the fee is $15. Anyone interested in more information on the stream may call Tim Hess at 804-325-2534. He will inform you of current hatches, the best fishing locations for your time of year, and the stocking situation.

TYE RIVER, NORTH FORK

Stream Type Freestone

Maps USGS Big Levels; DeLorme 54

Access Between Lexington and Staunton southbound, take exit 204 off I-81 and turn left on US 11. Travel to Steele's Tavern and turn right there on VA 56. Follow 56 east through Vesuvius and turn left on VA(s) 686. Turn off to the right onto VA(s) 687, which parallels the North Fork of the Tye River downstream.

Upstream, this relatively small water is posted with unmistakable NO FISH-ING signs. Four miles downstream from the intersection with VA(s) 687, there are some deep holes, with numerous small streams tumbling into the Tye from the mountains on either side. The water, which gives new meaning to the word *pure,* is crystal clear even in midsummer, maintaining a fairly good flow during the hot, dry months. In shaded pools, particularly

Tammy Hiner demonstrates her fly-fishing skill.

where feeder streams empty in, there is a good chance of running into native brook trout.

Along VA(s) 687 there are numerous slick-worn paths leading to the greener, deeper holes, and there's no doubt they have been fished heavily. Perhaps the saving feature of the Tye is its tendency to drop suddenly into a series of gorges hundreds of feet beneath the roadbed. At these places the stream becomes nearly inaccessible. Only someone with the time to fish into these ravines—or the daring to hand-over-hand down into them—will benefit from the mature brook trout here. The stream is no longer stocked.

The stream is filled with a mixed bag of minnows, which fight over your smaller flies for the privilege of hooking themselves. An overturned rock yields several types of nymphs of surprising size, and for some reason there is an absence of stonefly larvae. A Hare's Ear nymph comes closest to replicating the live forms found here.

About 5 miles downstream you run through a row of summer cabins barricaded with POSTED signs. This may pose a problem, because most of this property is absentee-owned, and thus it can be impossible to receive permission to fish. VA(s) 687 eventually merges with US 56, and following the road east takes you alongside a segment of the Tye that is 30 to 40 feet across. The stream is stocked alongside the pavement but flows rather slowly and would appear to be a little warm for trout after mid-June.

5 | Roanoke Valley

The city of Roanoke's claim to be Trout Capital of Virginia is based upon geography rather than the proximity of premier streams. There are fishable streams nearby, one being the Roanoke River, which has been cleaned up sufficiently to produce downtown rainbow trout. And within an hour's drive of the city limits there is considerable stocked stream mileage on waters such as Jennings, Potts, Barbour's, and the privately managed Cascades Creek, plus some lesser-known wild trout fisheries. Most of these suffer from their proximity to dense population, and in the spring Jennings Creek sees a dozen anglers perched upon boulders around their common favorite hole, glowering at one another. But drive for 2 or 3 hours, and you're on the banks of streams with few or no boot-trampled areas.

The 500-mile eastern flank of the southern Appalachians, better known as the Blue Ridge, drapes down from Pennsylvania Amish country all the way into northern Georgia. If it were a diamond necklace, its central pendant would be the Roanoke Valley. The Blue Ridge Parkway grazes the edge of the Roanoke city limits, and from it small gorges and ravines may be reached. Flowing through them are laurel-shaded waterways where mayflies hatch 7 months of the year.

Some but not all of these waters are covered in the section below. If you're looking for wild trout fly-fishing at its purest, one good way to find it is to trace the popular stocked streams up toward their sources. Here the angling traffic thins out, the litter line ends, and for those with a taste for small mountain-brook fishing, these freestone headwaters offer some challenging miniature plunge pools and rapids.

DAN RIVER

Stream Type Freestone
Maps USGS Meadows of Dan; DeLorme 25

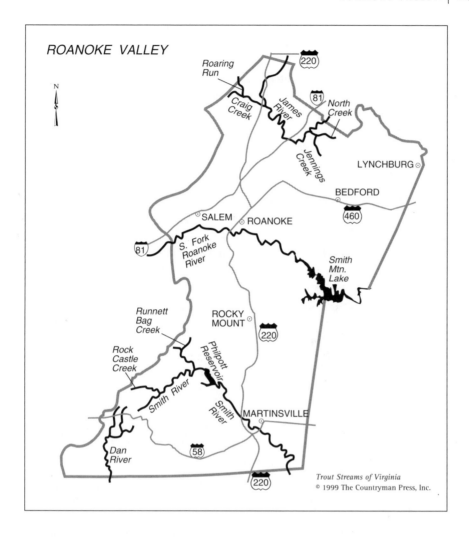

ROANOKE VALLEY

N

Roaring
Run

220

Craig
Creek

James
River

81

North
Creek

Jennings
Creek

LYNCHBURG

BEDFORD

460

SALEM ROANOKE

81

S. Fork
Roanoke
River

Smith
Mtn.
Lake

Runnett
Bag
Creek

ROCKY
MOUNT

220

Rock
Castle
Creek

Philpott
Reservoir

Smith River

Smith
River

MARTINSVILLE

Dan
River

58

220

Trout Streams of Virginia
© 1999 The Countryman Press, Inc.

Access On the Blue Ridge Parkway, just south of Meadows of Dan, turn south at milepost 184 onto VA(s) 614. Follow it through Bell Spur to VA(s) 631, turning left there. Route 631 becomes a gravel road leading to VA(s) 648, which is paved. Turn left on 648, and you will see the stocking signs along the Dan River. Stay on 648 until it dead-ends at the generating plant, where written permission to fish must be obtained. From there up the Pinnacles of Dan access is by footpath only.

The Dan is one of those unobtrusive streams one passes when driving through the area called Southside Virginia. For the most part it is a sluggish, silted, ditchlike stream flowing past occasional dilapidated clay-chinked log tobacco barns and not worth a second look. But turn upstream on VA(s) 648 and behold a slow miracle taking place. As you proceed toward the Pinnacles of Dan, the blowsy Dan River slowly upgrades its character to a clear, virginal stream more and more bespeaking trout.

This is a pattern repeated time after time with Appalachian trout fisheries. In the "flatlands" they mingle their original mountain source water with ingredients that would cause a carp to scarf: fertilizer, pesticides, cattle droppings, you name it. But the rewards of following even the most diseased rivers toward their sources can be dramatic. Often they become tumbling, blue-green and white fisheries that can hold you for a full day. The Dan is such a stream.

As VA 648 begins its climb into the foothills, rapids and swift pools appear. There is a vestige of silt, but it disappears as you go farther up the mountain, following the stream through wooded areas. Because of its ready accessibility from the roadside, the Dan remains a put-and-take stream lower down the mountainside. It's a comparatively large freestone river, averaging 75 to 100 feet across. At the base of the Pinnacles of Dan, there is a hydroelectric plant, and here the character of the Dan River changes dramatically.

Looking 2 miles up the alpine face of the Pinnacles, you can make out a thin black crescent, mottled with green. This is a power-generating dam, clinging to the mountainside, sending a flume underground to the generating plant. Down below is the two-story brick hydroelectric facility; behind it lies that half of the Dan River not captured by the underground flume, following the original streambed. In this unlikely setting is one of the more spectacular trout waters in southwest Virginia, with classic falls and deeps, containing green water occasionally disappearing into the black holes tunneled out by centuries of fast water.

Author's Note *On my first trip to the upper Dan River, I stopped at the generating plant to obtain written permission for fishing and to ask the length of the path leading upstream from the road's end. A lanky, bearded Patrick Countyan looked my sexagenarian physique up and down and replied, "As fur upstream as you wanta go." This turned out to be a total of 2 miles up the side of the Pinnacles.*

At the first Stoli-clear pool, I paused to observe four healthy brown trout sizing me up. At first they whipped around in the short, alert circle that usually lets me know I have been spotted and there's no way they'll take any lure. Since they soon returned and held in a steady pod, however, I tossed in a Muddler Minnow, which sent one of the four scurrying for a rock hideout. I tried another cast, dropping the Muddler just under their noses. One of them grabbed it, much to my surprise and that of his two companions, which streaked off in a hurry. The fish turned out to be a chunky brown, much heavier than his 14 inches would have indicated. Beautifully marked, he was bright gold all the way under his belly, with black circles defining magenta

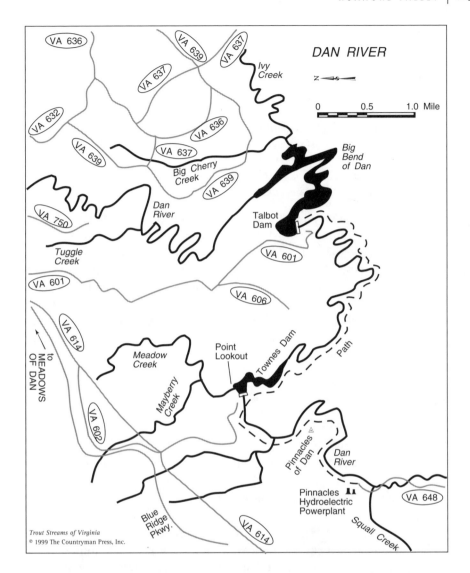

centers. *A brown trout maven later asked me if he was a German or Loch Leven, and I answered that I honestly didn't know. My experience with brown trout over the years has produced all manner of colors and designs, including star shapes, but the differences occurred in different streams, with different feeding patterns. There didn't seem to be any divided genealogies in any one stream.*

The next pool upstream produced another flash of gold, somewhat larger and cannier than the first. This fish was lying at the tail of a riffle, in shallow water, and at the sting of the hook immediately headed for a submerged bush. Burrowing into the leaves, he looked for a snag, apparently having been hooked before, perhaps a number of

*times. The bend of my rod finally generated enough pressure to pull
the hook free, and he disappeared in a flurry of twigs and leaves.*

*This particular visit was on a 60-degree day in December, 2 weeks
before Christmas. There was not a soul on the stream besides me,
and I saw not even a boot print, but plenty of insect life was flying.
Winter fishing conditions are the real beauty of trout angling in these
southern Appalachians, and for some it's the best season. At the
season's beginning, the road to the generating plant is one long parking lot, with people queuing up at their favorite holes. In December
the Dan is an exclusive club for one, shared with pods of friendly
browns, rainbows, and brookies.*

The rule of following streams up to their source until it hurts is particularly rewarding on the Dan. From the power plant to the first dam is a
comparatively easy 2-mile hike. Between the lower dam, Towne, and the
upper dam, Talbott, high on the side of the Pinnacles of Dan, the going gets
harder, with over 5 miles of excellent wild brook and rainbow fishing high
up on the side of the Pinnacles, alluring enough to keep an absorbed angler
stalking fish until dark through some difficult going. There are often plentiful midges over the water, and switching to a number 18 Black Wulff
sometimes proves a good choice.

JENNINGS CREEK

Stream Type Freestone

Maps USGS Arnold Valley; DeLorme 43, 53

Access Take exit 168 off I-81 and follow VA(s) 614 to Arcadia. On the way
you will cross a new concrete bridge that spans the James River. A reliable
local landmark is the Arcadia General Store.

One of the larger Virginia streams, the Jennings has one advantage, or
disadvantage, depending upon your viewpoint. It closely follows VA(s)
614, a paved road well known to local anglers. In fact, they can look out of
their vehicles and see if the fish are rising.

Later in the season, when bass are fishable, the Jennings quiets down
and becomes less of a put-and-take affair and more of a fly-fisher's domain.
The proximity of the James River, into which the Jennings flows, somewhat
filters out the bass-fishing crowd in June and July, and that's really the time
to see this stream at its best. Because of the meadows along its banks, floating hoppers may do well during warm-weather months. Toward dusk, a number 8 or 10 White Moth may snag one of the citation browns for which the
Jennings is famous. For rising fish the smaller-sized standard patterns may
be selected. Choose among the Coachman, Adams, Light Cahill, Hendrickson,
Blue Quill, Gray Fox, and Yellow Stonefly, depending upon the hatch.

So far we have been talking about the lower reaches of this stream. Upstream in the Jefferson National Forest, the Jennings becomes somewhat less of a social scene and more of a typical Appalachian spring creek. Its stream of origin is Fallingwater Creek, which aptly describes the terrain. Here it is possible to catch some small but energetic rainbow trout on black ants, nymphs, or a number 14 dry beetle.

Because of its multiple personality, the Jennings is a good candidate all season long. If the banks down in Arcadia are too crowded early in the season, you can just move higher up into the mountains and have the fishing all to yourself on the Jennings or its regulated tributary, North Creek.

In the fall, when the water temperature drops, downstream becomes the place to catch larger fish. And so far Virginia trout anglers are not taking full advantage of fall and winter fishing on the Jennings, which can be excellent at times.

NORTH CREEK

Stream Type Freestone

Maps USGS Arnold Valley; DeLorme 53

Special Regulations On the stretch of water just above the North Creek National Forest Campground and continuing to its headwaters, fishing is restricted to single-hook artificial lures; creel limit two fish at least 9 inches long per day; fishing must cease when creel limit is attained.

Access Take exit 168 off I-81 and follow VA(s) 614 to Arcadia. The road follows the larger Jennings Creek, into which North Creek flows—also good trout fishing although strictly put-and-take in the spring. It's always a good idea to stop at the Arcadia General Store and ask about the fishing, since the main clientele there are anglers and wardens. About a mile past the store, a sign directs you left onto a gravel road leading to the NORTH CREEK CAMPGROUND, and a regularly stocked section of the stream parallels the road here. This is an immaculately maintained stretch of North Creek, with frequent man-made weirs damming up smooth stretches of water.

Just upstream from the campground a sign indicates the mile of regulated section, and there are frequent parking pull-offs. This regulated stretch has been extended another half a mile. The road ends abruptly with the Appalachian Trail taking over. The walk up the trail to Apple Orchard Falls is worth the effort, as above the falls you may have an abundance of small but feisty native brookies all to yourself.

One frequent customer of the Orvis store in Roanoke fishes only North Creek, out of all the waters available to him. And a select number of other Old Dominion trout anglers have been heard to share this sentiment. Even a casual first look at this gemlike mountain stream hints that there is something special that attracts lovers of good trout water again and again.

Flowing through the Botetourt County section of Jefferson National Forest, North Creek tumbles through a mixture of hardwoods and hemlocks. Every couple of hundred yards a freshet of springwater hits the main channel, forming small but deep pools. Each stretch affords another fishing opportunity, plus a new delight to the eye. The abundance of springwater and shade keeps North Creek ideally cool for trout, even during midsummer. The mile-long regulated stretch is unstocked, and all the mostly wild rainbows reproduce naturally, fighting like the natives they really have become. With typically soft acid water, North Creek is a better habitat for brook trout than for the other species.

Healthy mayfly hatches may be observed rising from the pools, particularly sulphur duns with spinners. A number 16 imitation of this hatch can be productive. Since this is a steep-gradient forest stream, dry-fly fishing is limited to short stretches of smooth water. Any of a selection of smaller dark nymphs would be less frustrating to fish, along with black ants and Woolly Worms. It would be a safe guess that 90 percent of the diet here is nymphs.

The bank is somewhat crowded with mature trees, rather than bushes, making the backcast difficult. It is necessary to glance over your shoulder prior to the backward flip, making sure there is an opening between tree trunks. Even then a great deal of time will be spent sitting on a mossy hemlock root tying on a new fly. But the scenery more than compensates for the lost ties, and you may even be tempted to munch on an early-spring teaberry or two just to freshen your mouth.

It may seem paradoxical, but on this small stream, as on many other highland Virginia fisheries, a longer rod is preferable to some of the small, whippy models. With an 8-footer you can extend your leader upstream between limbs to hover above just the right stretch of tailwater. In some places you can cast by bending a longer rod into an arc by pulling back on the fly between your thumb and forefinger (carefully), releasing it, and catapulting the fly into just the right spot. This technique can be used to explore narrow enclaves passed up by other anglers but not by trout.

ROANOKE RIVER

Stream Type Limestone

Maps USGS Elliston; DeLorme 41, 42

Access To reach the South Fork of the Roanoke River, from I-81 turn off at the Dixie Caverns exit. Follow US 11/460 south into Shawsville. At the Meadowbrook Retirement Home turn left on VA(s) 637, which follows the stream all the way to its source.

The story of this stream is a marvel of reclamation rather than of angling excellence. Meandering through the edge of downtown Roanoke, it is far from one of Virginia's premier trout streams, but 50 years ago it was the color and consistency of green liquid soap, supporting a few hardy mudcats, carrying all the effluvia of an open sewer. Today anglers in chest waders fish in the shadow of Veteran's Stadium, catching stocked fish. Hypothetically, a surgeon in Roanoke's largest hospital could walk out of the emergency room entrance in waders and vest and be fishing in 2 minutes. Happy-faced kids can be seen in the spring, walking up from Wasena Park with limits of rainbows. Upstream near the city of Salem, the river has an Avon-like quality with colonies of mallards waddling across grassy banks.

In order to fairly evaluate the Roanoke as a trout stream, one should drive north of Salem down US 11 past Shawsville. There the Roanoke completely changes character from a placid river to a tumbling mountain stream, with Bony's Run and Dark Run infusing it with cold springwater year-round. Most of it is bordered by private land, prominently marked with POSTED signs. However, access to stretches of trout water along the South Fork may be identified by signs showing where stocking took place. Eventually in Floyd County the Roanoke becomes Purgatory Creek, no longer a river but now a series of falls, riffles, and small pools flowing down the side of Lick Ridge.

The relatively few designated fishing areas tend to be crowded early in the season. Later on in June and July you won't find quite as many boot tracks, and this is the time to try an assortment of nymphs, black ants, and streamers. Upstream of Shawsville dry flies are difficult to fish because of the predominant rapids, but an Adams number 20 may be dipped in the occasional enclaves of quiet water.

Downstream near the city it's a different story, with bathtublike stretches hundreds of yards long for floating a fly. The trouble here is fishing pressure from Roanokers, who can change after work and get in a couple of hours of angling before dark. Holding out are a few suspicious brown trout that ignore the bait and spinners, hiding under the bank until late twilight. Large White Moths or Mosquitoes might lure one of these wily monsters out of hiding late in the evening, but it's far from a sure bet.

ROARING RUN

Stream Type Limestone

Maps USGS Strom; DeLorme 52

Access Turning off US 220 onto VA(s) 615 takes you alongside Craig Creek, which empties into the James River at the intersection. Upstream you encounter Roaring Run crossing the road at VA(s) 621. The turnoff is well marked by a national forest sign reading ROARING RUN. A short distance later state stocking signs mark the trees.

This is a mountain stream just within the boundary of the Jefferson National Forest. A high-banked steep-gradient stream with cascades and potholes, Roaring Run invites wet-fly and nymph fishing.

The stream banks are steep rock walls covered for the most part with damp moss. Occasional bare pine roots serve as convenient grab bars for those in need of such assistance. Mostly the water consists of heavy current, deep pools, and infrequent quiet stretches where fish may be observed rising to mayfly hatches. The early hatch seems to be light cahills, with a few olive-blue dun flies. There are a variety of other aquatic insects flying about the stream as well, so turn over some stones to check the nymph population before making your choice of lure.

Be prepared for heavy fishing traffic on Roaring Run, since despite its unspoiled appearance, the stream is paralleled by a well-maintained gravel road. It is close to population centers, and its reputation as a trout producer is well known by local anglers. Frequent whole-kernel corn cans and empty salmon-egg jars remind us of the job still remaining for Trout Unlimited and other concerned troutists.

There are still some old-timers around who can remember when Roaring Run was a wilderness stream, to be experienced only by those hardy enough to pack in a tent, army cots, cast-iron skillet, and enough bacon, eggs, and beans to accompany the week's catch of fat brook trout. That Roaring Run is gone and can never be more than a memory.

At the end of the gravel road there is a well-manicured picnic ground on the site of a pre–Civil War iron furnace dating back to 1838. It is possible, if you walk upstream far enough, to recapture a little of the wilderness that once surrounded Roaring Run. This upper stretch is barred to motorized traffic, which thins out the less hardy. It does take some walking through moderately difficult terrain to reach wild rainbow territory.

Walking upstream above the old furnace can provide the connoisseur of wild trout fishing the essence of that sport. Although the lower section remains put-and-take stocked water, a 1-mile trophy trout section has been established between the third footbridge and the Botetourt County line. Trout growth and survival of the stocked brown and rainbow fingerlings has been excellent, with trout exceeding 13 inches are available for catch-and-release anglers. The paths are increasingly less beaten down as you proceed upstream, so you might consider saving your serious fishing time for this area.

ROCK CASTLE CREEK

Stream Type Freestone

Maps USGS Woolwine; DeLorme 25

Access Exit the Blue Ridge Parkway at Tuggle Gap and take VA 8 south, turning left on VA(s) 678 just north of the village of Woolwine. This takes you to the stocked section of Rock Castle Creek. A right turn on VA(s) 837 brings you parallel to a rhododendron-bordered area of the stream and, after a half mile, a dead end.

Rock Castle Creek flows through red-clay country in Patrick County, which adjoins Henry County. And like the fiery patriot and sworn foe of the Constitution who once governed these hills and whose namesake the counties are, the Rock Castle is somewhat of a paradox and a mystery. It has all the attributes of a productive Virginia mountain stream: frequent spring creeks feeding in cold water, an average 30-foot width of rapids with pools below, state stocking that indicates promising trout habitat, plenty of aquatic-insect life, and a good gravel-and-sand bottom. So what's the paradox? In spite of a remoteness that eliminates the slick-worn paths decorated with boot tracks, the hatches go undisturbed and fish are not easily spotted.

One might still be tempted to say this is a put-and-take stream with bruising traffic on the weekends, but that doesn't really seem to be the case. Sure, there is some evidence of bait-fishermen, but the Rock Castle is the type of habitat that should be able to withstand moderate pressure. There don't appear to be many mayflies, but there are prolific midges and terrestrials. One possible solution to the mystery is the abundance of minnows, snails, and other underwater life-forms. Turning over stones produces a stonefly larva or two, but no mayfly nymphs.

As for wet flies, a Muddler Minnow can produce some strikes, but they appear to be rainbow fingerlings, 6 inches or less. Starting halfway down VA(s) 837 and working upstream takes you through some reasonably attractive water. Under the VA(s) 837 bridge the water becomes deeper, and just above it there is a natural dam with green water under the falls. Farther along you find a still stretch relatively free of foliage, where dry flies may be floated naturally near huge sycamore stumps.

Then the overhanging vegetation takes over, and you may hang your hook in a selection of maple, spicewood, rhododendron, sycamore, and other brush on every other backcast. Another distraction for the newcomer is the "gold" shining on the bottom—fool's gold or iron pyrite, of course, but flashing in the sun the particles look more like high-grade ore than the real thing does. This is also iron country, as evidenced by the brick color of the streambed and water that has a slightly ferrous odor and appearance. These mineral characteristics also exist in neighboring streams, like the Smith River, which some call the top trout stream in Virginia.

Add another paradox: The farther upstream you fish, the deeper the water appears to be, probably due to the high banks channeling the stream more closely. Up the mountainside approaching the Blue Ridge Parkway, the sand-and-gravel bottom gives way to stone, channeling rapids into plunge pools holding small brook trout. But this part of the stream without a doubt also holds some wise old heavy-bodied rainbows, though it's going to take some careful checkmate planning to unravel their secrets and penetrate their hideouts, with rapid-fire changes of lure until the bug of the day is finally served up.

It may take more than one visit to the Rock Castle to fully unravel its mysteries, but it's worth a return trip. Or better yet, first find that rare species, fly-anglers familiar with the stream who are also willing to speak of its secrets. They might even give away the existence of excellent wild trout fishing if you go upstream far enough. Good luck!

RUNNETT BAG CREEK

Stream Type Freestone

Maps USGS Endicott; DeLorme 26

Access Driving south of Roanoke on the Blue Ridge Parkway to just past Smart View Park, turn left on VA(s) 793. This takes you off the crest of the Blue Ridge Mountains, down a gravel road that parallels Runnett Bag Creek and eventually leads to pavement.

Runnett Bag Creek is for the most part a gentle-gradient stream, averaging 20 feet in width. Even in the low-water months it maintains a fair volume. Because of a heavy overgrowth of brush it is advisable to wade the streambed rather than attempt to hike along the banks. There is a proliferation of terrestrials, including grasshoppers, crickets, spiders, and beetles. The stream bottom tends to silt over, however, and some of the more inviting holes heat up too much in the summer for holdover trout.

State trout-stocking signs show up after the road emerges from a heavily timbered area, and they continue for approximately 2 miles off the paved road. Access to the stream is through private lanes turning west off the highway. Where VA(s) 818 turns right off VA(s) 793 there is a wooden bridge with fairly deep water beneath it alive with minnows and larger coarse fish. A week or two after one of Virginia's unannounced stockings would be the best time to try some small patterns such as an Adams or Coachman number 14.

The Runnett Bag is one of those streams close to population centers that present some fishing in early spring and during Indian summer. A gentle gradient plus abundant fine sand on the bottom make it, for the most part, an unproductive warm-weather fishery. One exception is the series of rapids behind the Endicott Assembly Church, where there is a fairly steep drop. The stream spills over log-and-brush dams into well-oxygenated pools below, holding whatever wild rainbows survive through the summer.

Along the dirt stretch of VA(s) 793 leading down from the Blue Ridge Parkway there is evidence of heavy timber cutting, which may explain why the Runnett Bag has a cloudy look even when there have been no recent rains. This is an unstocked area, and though little more than a rivulet, it holds a few natives that can be spotted scurrying for cover. All of this timbered area is private property, and care should be taken to obtain permission to fish.

A typical sight in Runnett Bag Valley is an older citizen wearing gallus overalls and a John Deere or Caterpillar hat, walking along the road. These are friendly people, eager to talk and ready to admit they were makers of illegal whiskey during Prohibition. In fact, it is grudgingly recorded that Franklin County was the champion producer of moonshine even into the 1930s. At one time during the 1920s, records show it led all U.S. counties in its purchase of refined sugar by the ton.

Some of the region's younger inhabitants have adopted to an alarming degree the easier and more lucrative growing of marijuana as a substitute for bootlegging. These pot farmers are not such friendly people, and one state trooper reports finding fishhooks suspended on monofilament at eye level above the trail in an area south of here. Luckily, he spotted them in time. If you glimpse a clearing along the stream bank displaying clusters of cannabis's characteristic spear-shaped leaves, instant departure is advised, and the same is probably good advice to those fishing any remote area of the country nowadays.

SMITH RIVER

Stream Type Freestone (lower tailwater)

Maps USGS Bassett, Philpott Lake; DeLorme 26

Special Regulations Beginning just below the confluence of Town Creek and the Smith, and extending about 3 miles down the VA(s) 666 bridge, fishing is restricted to single-hook artificial flies; creel limit is two fish per day, 16 inches or better; all fish less than 16 inches must be handled carefully and immediately returned unharmed to the water; possession of fish less than 16 inches on this water is illegal; possession of bait on this water is illegal. Fishing is permitted year-round.

Access Turn west off US 220 at Oak Level. Follow VA(s) 674 all the way to

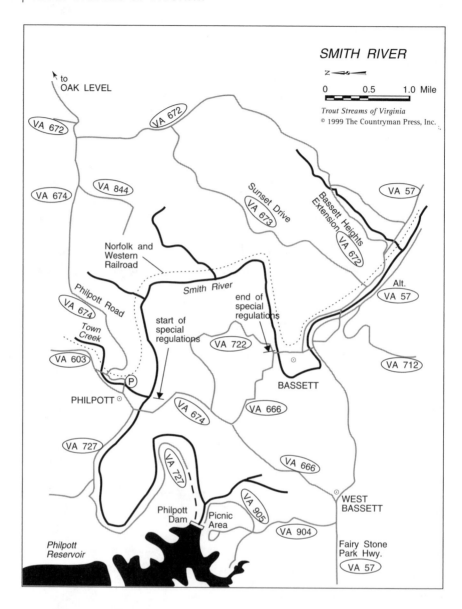

SMITH RIVER

N

0   0.5   1.0 Mile

Trout Streams of Virginia
© 1999 The Countryman Press, Inc.

to OAK LEVEL

VA 672

VA 672

VA 844

VA 674

VA 57

Sunset Drive
VA 673

Bassett Heights Extension VA 672

Norfolk and Western Railroad

Smith River

Alt. VA 57

Philpott Road

VA 674

end of special regulations

Town Creek

start of special regulations

VA 722

VA 603

VA 712

P

BASSETT

PHILPOTT

VA 674

VA 666

VA 727

VA 727

VA 666

WEST BASSETT

Philpott Dam

Picnic Area

VA 905

VA 904

Philpott Reservoir

Fairy Stone Park Hwy.
VA 57

the Norfolk & Western Railroad paralleling the river. Some words of caution: Just past Oak Level, there is a right turn on 674 that looks like another road intersecting at 90 degrees and is thus easy to miss. At the railroad crossing, continue straight ahead to a parking area. Only walking is permitted down the access road into the special-regulations area.

In the unlikely event that Mother Nature and the Corps of Engineers were to collaborate on designing a fly-fishing stream, it would end up looking a lot like the Smith River. Its run-riffle-pool habitat is ideal for king-sized browns, one of which is in the record book as the state's largest. Chances are better that you'll catch a goodly number of 10- to 12-inchers, although an occasional mammoth old wary brown may be seen cruising the banks. While the state stocks large numbers of rainbows, the Smith is best known for stream-bred browns. Reproduction takes place in late November from just below Philpott Dam down through the community of Stanleytown.

The stream widens to over 100 feet in some places along the lower stretch. Although it's big water, hip waders will do fine, as shallow riffles frequently parallel deep pools on the opposite bank. There's some gravel and sand for good footing, but enough stretches of shelf rock to require felt-soled waders. The Smith is also consistently cold, so a dunking is uncomfortable at almost any time of year.

Once a smallmouth river typical of the Blue Ridge foothills, the Smith changed drastically with the building of Philpott Dam in the early 1950s to become the first of Virginia's premier tailwater trout streams. Because the water used for power generation comes from the 200-foot-deep bottom, the temperature hovers at around 45 degrees at the tailrace. From there it flows through 15 miles of trout water.

Occasionally, the river's bucolic peace is ripped by the sound of a siren from Philpott Dam. Get out of the water immediately, as a dangerous 3-foot torrent of water soon follows. Approaching high water, flows increase from below 100 cfs (cubic feet per second) to over 1,500 cfs. Make a point of checking on generating times before traveling to the Smith. The Corps of Engineers sets a schedule for release times, which may be obtained by calling for a prerecorded message at 276-629-2432. There is usually no generation on weekends, and activity during the week depends on rainfall and electrical demand. After generation release stops, it may take an hour and a half for the water to subside to an ideal fishing level. The Corps of Engineers cooperates with anglers on releases, although they caution that their release times are not absolutely accurate. We may occasionally resent the inconvenience of the water releases, but the fact is that without the cooling effect of the dam, this freestone stream would not be the brown trout fishery it is, particularly in midsummer.

Much of the riverbank displays rhododendron overhanging deep undercuts. Sizable trout may be seen feeding in these areas, usually on terrestrials dropping from the branches. A black ant placed upstream to drift just under the boughs can often get a rise. These larger fish have seen just about every fly tied, so the smaller the pattern, the better. And using a number 7 tippet may be worth all the fussy little twists and tangles it can produce.

The regulated portion of the Smith is catch-and-release for all but two 16-inch or better fish. But there are enough large fish to make that a meaningful limit. One local fisherman marks off 16 inches on his upper arm with a Magic Marker, saving the trouble of packing a ruler. Many other responsible anglers return all fish, regardless of size.

This stream has developed quite a national reputation, and, occasionally, license plates from Vermont or Wyoming can be seen. However far you have to travel, the mileage is worth the fun of a day's casting on the Smith. One aspect outsiders must get used to is the "gold" sprinkled along the river bottom. No matter how nuggetlike they may look, the "high-grade" particles always turn out to be pieces of mica reflecting the sun. You might as well concentrate on the true gold reflecting from the sides of beautifully tinted brown trout.

As with any tailwater, you will find the fish more active just below the dam during winter months. This is because the trout living here are more accustomed to constant cold temperatures than the fish living downstream, where temperatures fluctuate between summer and winter.

The regulated stretch runs from Town Creek to Bassett and is vintage Appalachian. Flights of mallards often tip overhead, and an occasional great blue heron grudgingly spreads its 4-foot wings. A wonderful swarm of sulphurs, the best known of Smith River hatches, often triggers a feeding frenzy on a May or June evening when shadberry trees begin to bloom. Size 18 is recommended. Along with the sulphurs, a goodly number of march browns and hendricksons adds to the excitement. During the summer months, feeding activity centers mainly on terrestrials such as ants, beetles, crickets, and hoppers. In early fall, in addition to the terrestrials, caddis begin to emerge along with some of the larger blue-winged olives. The late-fall and winter blue-wings are somewhat smaller and less abundant. In the absence of cold-weather hatches, streamers and nymphs fished very slowly prove effective.

The best hatches occur immediately below the inflow of Town Creek, which adds nutrients to the water. Town is also the beginning of the special-regulations area where only artificial lures may be used. The area north of the stocked section was previously closed but may now be fished year-round, giving an added bonus to Smith River anglers.

In addition to the regulated section described here, there is excellent wild brown trout fishing all the way from the dam to Martinsville.

6 | New River Drainage Area

The New River is deceptively named, being the second-oldest river in the world next to the Nile. Rising in western North Carolina, it runs northeast and then north through Virginia, skirting the West Virginia border. At Gauley Bridge, West Virginia, it joins the Gauley River to form the Kanawha, which is part of the Ohio River watershed. It has the distinction of being the only surviving ancient river that rises in the Blue Ridge, cuts west through the mountains, and eventually supplies water to the Mississippi and the Gulf of Mexico. The icy water of its tributary the Little Stony, spilling over your hip waders, will eventually lap the shores of Veracruz.

The New shapes the look of the land surrounding it, in some areas being a flat half mile across, dotted with anglers wading it knee-deep, spin-fishing for redeyes. Winding back upon itself, the river dips between mountains and becomes narrow, deep walleye water. Freestone streams like the regulated stretch of Little Stony Creek plunge down the mountainsides toward the New River gorges, pausing just long enough for prime mayfly hatches.

BARBOUR'S CREEK (JAMES RIVER DRAINAGE)

Stream Type Freestone

Maps USGS Newscastle; DeLorme 52

Access From Newcastle take VA(s) 615 to the east out of town. Turn left on VA(s) 609 until it dead-ends into VA(s) 611. At 611 one may go either left upstream or right downstream. The stream averages from 15 to 20 feet wide and is relatively shallow. There are a couple of miles of private land, heavily posted. Turning right off 611 onto 617, one eventually reaches the Jefferson National Forest campground called the Pines.

All along VA(s) 617 Barbour's Creek is relatively small, with signs indicating it is stocked by the state. Farther upstream you enter what is

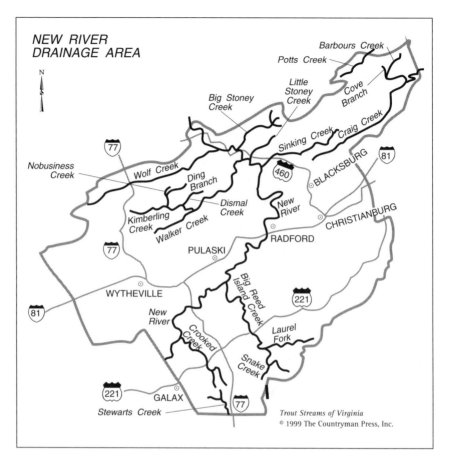

NEW RIVER
DRAINAGE AREA

N

Barbours Creek

Potts Creek

Little
Stoney
Creek

Cove
Branch

Big Stoney
Creek

Sinking Creek

Craig Creek

BLACKSBURG

81

Nobusiness
Creek

Wolf Creek

Ding
Branch

460

Dismal
Creek

New
River

CHRISTIANBURG

Kimberling
Creek

Walker Creek

RADFORD

77

PULASKI

Big Reed
Island Creek

WYTHEVILLE

221

81

New
River

Crooked
Creek

Laurel
Fork

Snake
Creek

221

GALAX

77

Stewarts Creek

Trout Streams of Virginia
© 1999 The Countryman Press, Inc.

called the National Forest Wilderness Area. Here the stream may be reached by a series of one-lane dirt forestry roads by going either right or left, as the stream crosses the highway frequently.

Above the Pines Campground and the Horse Corral, the stream gradient becomes somewhat steeper, transforming Barbour's Creek into a series of small cascades with deep green grottoes beneath them. These deeper spots hold a number of trout hiding among the rocks at the stream bottom. The lower reaches offer wild brown and brook trout fishing, while the North Fork headwaters is strictly wild brook trout habitat.

Barbour's is one of the Craig County streams that enjoyed an early reputation as one of Virginia's finer trout fisheries. In recent years the stream has gone downhill somewhat, due to overfishing plus habitat destruction by floods. The stream is still good trout habitat, however, and has the potential for restoration with more of the careful management it's receiving. Flies that do well here are the Adams number 14, Hare's Ear nymphs, Wulff patterns, and variations of the Coachman.

BIG STONY CREEK

Stream Type Freestone

Maps USGS Lindside; DeLorme 41

Access Take I-81 south from Roanoke, follow exit 118 at Christiansburg, and take US 460 west from Blacksburg. Passing through Pembroke, go 2 miles and take VA(s) 635 right. This road takes you into the Jefferson National Forest, where the signs indicate stocked water. Three miles upstream you enter an area lined with private cabins, but there is access for fishing here.

A round the footbridge taking the Appalachian Trail across Big Stony, the terrain levels out appreciably. The rapids are consequently less swift and the holes not as deep. It is good trout water, with somewhat less pressure than the more scenic sections downstream. Because of the water's slower pace, there is a growth of algae on the streambed, and flat stones can be unavoidably slick, so choose your footing carefully and take advantage of the handholds afforded by overhanging rhododendron.

There is an excellent national forest campground at White Rocks, where leaders can be repaired, lunch eaten, or serious contemplation undertaken. There may be interruptions from the unruly population of red squirrels here, which specialize in peanut butter sandwich remnants.

Lower down, there are some quiet pools where rising fish may be spotted in midafternoon. A number 18 or 20 Adams fly may prove effective. Hatches of quill gordons have been observed here in April.

Big Stony is one of Virginia's better-publicized streams, with nearly 6 miles of heavily fished water. Because of the nooks and crannies afforded by its big stones, it can hold fish despite the heavy early-season pressure. In addition to a good holdover population, the stream contains a fair number of wild browns and brookies. But these are lure-wary trout, requiring many selections of flies before the right combination is found. And some careful stalking behind the demanding rhododendron cover doesn't hurt either.

During Virginia's spring turkey season, a hunting break may be a pleasant midmorning distraction when the fishing slows down. Following feeder routes to the Appalachian Trail, you'll have only a short walk from the Big Stony to heavy turkey scratchings. One of the ironies of gobbler hunting here is the likelihood of finding a truly virgin mountain-spring creek. As you part the laurel with a gun barrel, you may see a tiny stream's mirror surface broken by 8 or 10 native brookies of indeterminate size. And then, wouldn't you know, later in the afternoon the fishing may be interrupted by a couple of pterodactyl-sized turkeys overhead cruising the stream.

CRAIG CREEK (JAMES RIVER DRAINAGE)

Stream Type Freestone

Maps USGS McDonald's Mill; DeLorme 41

Access Take I-81 exit 140 at Salem; go north on VA 311. Turn left on VA(s) 621 and follow it to the Craig–Montgomery county line. Proceed to a national forest area sign, CALDWELL FIELDS, and go upstream about 2 miles from there. Trout-stocking signs are posted, but some of the more interesting dirt roads lead to unstocked areas.

Anyone looking for beaucoup trout in plenty of water might as well stay away from the headwaters of Craig Creek. But the student of trout interested in seeing a small display case of mountain-stream habitat will be handsomely rewarded by this stream.

Local residents know Craig Creek as a bass fishery, with its wide, meadow-bordered waters inhabited by an assortment of pickerel, perch, and rough fish. This is the Craig County face of the stream. But across the Montgomery county line it assumes another identity altogether. Here in glassy little pools the microcosmic infant Craig Creek trickles along under massive rock cliffs and through laurel and rhododendron glens. This is one of those just-for-fun streams, shallower for the most part than your ankle bone. An occasional chest-deep pool will hold a family of five or six 14-inch holdover stocked trout gazing up with disarming innocence. You can sit on a carpet of pine needles and observe them going about their daily business, mostly feeding on gnats, ants, and small beetles. Any movement on your part will cause mild alarm, sending the fish meandering to crevices in rocks and sunken logs.

Fishing this stretch of the stream is a matter of outwitting these small families of brookies and rainbows by wearing camouflage clothing, using natural cover, and tying plenty of 5X or smaller leader to number 20 terrestrials. Success is directly proportional to patience, as once these trout see you above their glassy pool, there's little chance of their taking your fly. So be prepared for much slow and careful stalking behind natural cover.

It is to be hoped that all those fishing this pearl of a stream will realize what a delicate crucible of life it really is. These are amazing fish, heavy and healthy looking, making the most of what food is available to them. Watching them go about their daily business affords a streamside classroom in trout ecology, with water so clear you can see the bottom from 50 feet away. The experience gives one a feel for how wild trout thrived in this country for millennia before there was need for a stocking program. It proves that a step-across brook really is capable of supporting decent-sized trout as long as human greed doesn't catch up with them. How many of these survivors you can catch is unimportant compared to how many you

Lew Thurman, a retired banker and noted maker of split-bamboo rods, fishes a limestone creek in Craig County.

can release back into their small universe. We hope there are enough people around who like to see trout in a trout stream to conserve this family.

CROOKED CREEK

Stream Type Freestone

Maps USGS Woodlawn; DeLorme 24

Special Regulations Crooked Creek and its tributaries are fee-fishing water: a daily permit costing $4.00 is required in addition to a Virginia fishing license. The permit can be obtained at the refreshment area and must be signed by the licensee. Creel limit is six trout per day; the season runs from 9 AM on the first Saturday in April through January 31 (note that a fee permit is not required after Labor Day, although a Virginia trout stamp is); daily fishing hours are 7 AM to 6 PM in March and April, and 6 AM to 7 PM May through September.

Access From I-81, turn south onto I-77 and follow it to the Hillsville exit. Get on US 221 south for 3 miles to VA(s) 620; turn left and go 3 miles to reach the East Fork. This is a small county road that dribbles away into a dirt lane. Don't become discouraged, as along the way there are prominent road signs showing the way to Crooked Creek. For those more leisurely travelers following the Blue Ridge Parkway, take the Meadows of Dan exit for US 58 north to Hillsville. Then turn south on US 221 and follow the above directions.

The Crooked Creek Wildlife Management Area holds within its borders approximately 7 miles of trout streams. The Virginia Department of Game and Inland Fisheries maintains holding tanks on the premises, from which the waters are stocked 4 days a week. This unique experiment by the state is a veritable supermarket of angling. You might say there is something here for trout anglers of every persuasion: quiet pools flowing through a meadow behind the parking lot; moderately riffled areas running through a small gorge, all heavily stocked; and for the fly-flickers, the best bet is the East Fork of Crooked Creek, an area of native brook trout only, no stocking. It is recommended you allot at least a full day to explore the fishing here. Two days would be even better.

Trout here run the gamut from native brookies, which fight like fish twice their size, through freshly stocked rainbows barely weaned off Purina Trout Chow, to 8-pound browns brooding for years in dark pockets beneath the banks. Since this is a game-management area as well as a managed fishery, anglers are likely to see a king turkey gobbler and his harem drinking from the creek, or a herd of deer at twilight packed into a small mountain meadow. Frequently you will run across deserted cadavers of frame houses that once housed hardscrabble farmers and their families when it was possible for them to make a living in areas such as this.

To fish the East Fork of Crooked Creek, drive to the holding tanks and park in a designated area. Then cross the stream and follow the right-hand fork to the dam. Next do some ridge running a short distance upstream to the unstocked area, where privacy is guaranteed, except for some exceptionally feisty wild brookies.

This is vintage Appalachian stream fishing, with 10-foot canopies of rhododendron kissing the stream. Be prepared for your fly to catch on the branches and leaves of these attractive but unyielding bushes. And another tip: Don't try any cross-country shortcuts to another section of the stream.

The rhododendron jungle, rivaling any mangrove forest, stretches on for hundreds of acres of totally confusing maze. Stick to wading and you'll avoid the crush.

This is a stream for small nymphs and streamers, cast a few feet up a fall and allowed to drift back down into the hole beneath. Take a good assortment of small terrestrials as well, and watch to see what's dropping off the overhang. A number 18 black ant can be dapped from an 8-foot rod on just 10 or so feet of line out, with a good concealing boulder in front of you. Moderately good hatches of dark cahills have been seen emerging on the East Fork, with plenty of winged ants clambering over the boulders.

Frankly, these fish, like all natives, are fickle. If they don't choose to feed at your designated time, forget it. No amount of fly-changing or streamside tying to match the hatch will be effective. They will follow your

Steve and Tammy Hiner collect insects on a Craig County stream.

fly in droves and inevitably turn away at the last moment. And just as suddenly they will start feeding, striking nearly everything.

DISMAL CREEK

Stream Type Freestone

Maps USGS Mechanicsburg; DeLorme 40

Access From I-81 take exit 98 onto VA 100 north past Dublin. From 100 turn west (left) onto VA 42 near Poplar Hill. Follow 42 through White Gate to VA(s) 606 and turn north (right). You will cross Dismal Creek at the sawmill on the left and take the next right, following the Dismal upstream. A dirt road turns off and dead-ends at Dismal Falls, where your vehicle may be parked.

It's not too difficult to imagine a cartographer at the turn of the 19th century suddenly coming upon a stream in the "Deep Woods" (an old name for Virginia). Perhaps the November wind is whipping a few snowflakes onto the water and it's getting dark enough to make camp. Unrolling his parchment, this buckskin-clad place-namer wrote "Creek" next to the meandering stream line he had just drawn. Pondering for a moment while looking at the dark bellies of early-winter clouds, he added "Dismal." To all those travelers who followed his map, headed west on the Wilderness Road, this stream was "The Dismal." And so it remains to this day.

On a spring morning when the sunlight is just beginning to dance off its riffles, the last word any trout seeker of today would use to describe this stream is *dismal—delightful,* perhaps, or *distracting,* but never *dismal.* On the opposite bank there is an occasional glimpse of the Appalachian Trail, which may be reached by a log bridge. The quiet might be broken by a grouse exploded from the greenbriers by the unnatural flapping of hip waders.

This lower stretch is deep and rapid, with healthy trout favoring undercut holes beside the bank. If you're fishing from midstream, casts can be directed to the right or left with equal success. This is a wet-fly stream, although the chorus of dry-fly purists may disagree. Start with a March Brown number 10, or a Light Cahill number 14 nymph, depending upon what is clinging to the stones. Take some time to observe which edible insects are dropping from the overhanging vegetation. Sometimes changing to a shiny green beetle can whet a big brown's appetite. A Hare's Ear offers some variety when none of these is working for you.

Above the falls there is a dense wall of laurel and greenbriers intermingled, with glassy-slick rocks underfoot. There are holdover fish here, no doubt because of the impossible casting conditions; you find yourself hanging on to a laurel limb and trying to find a hole large enough even to accommodate your rod tip. This *could* get dismal.

A better idea would be to bypass the wall of vegetation by driving upstream to the White Pine Horse Camp, where a smaller but more inviting version of the stream beckons. Here there is open country, much more sunlight reaching the water, and the possibility of finding a hatch of green drakes or maybe some terrestrials such as black jassids or flying ants. Large stretches of the Dismal do dry up during periods of extreme drought.

This corner of the Jefferson National Forest is also home to virtually unknown little trout havens such as Nobusiness Creek and Ding Branch—worth exploring although not worth a detailed description in this book. Checking a map of the local area will reveal a rich network of these small branches, not necessarily tributaries of Dismal Creek.

HELTON CREEK

Stream Type Freestone

Maps USGS Whitetop Mountain; DeLorme 22, 23

Access From I-81 take exit 45 onto VA 16 south. At the intersection at Volney take VA 58 west, past Grayson Highlands State Park, to VA(s) 783, a dirt road turning off to the right and following Helton Creek to its source.

Helton Creek is a moderately small but picturesque stream, stocked at the lower end. Above the Upper Helton Baptist Church it's surrounded by private property, although no POSTED signs are apparent. One small corner of Jefferson National Forest crosses it here. Despite the frequency of small farms, Helton Creek preserves its identity pretty well. Higher up, it narrows to about half its downstream size, becoming a native trout habitat.

Lower down, where the Helton is markedly wider, it also drops at a steeper gradient. Boulders in the streambed are smaller than in other local streams and therefore don't offer the angler as much cover. In the steeper portion there are a number of pools, but none of these appears to be more than 6 feet deep.

This stream is the type one might include as a summertime side trip when action on the nearby Whitetop Laurel or Big Wilson slows down. The lower temperature of its headwaters may provide action when warmer pools on the large streams do not.

LAUREL FORK (CARROLL COUNTY)

Stream Type Freestone

Maps USGS Laurel Fork; DeLorme 25

Access From the Blue Ridge Parkway, take the Meadows of Dan exit to VA 58 west to the village of Laurel Fork. Turn right onto County Road 638, following it several miles to where VA(s) 628 turns to the left and parallels Burk's Fork. Take another left at VA(s) 660, following it south to VA(s) 664, turning right there and following 664 for 0.5 mile. Then take VA(s) 661 to the left, follow it 0.5 mile—and here's where it gets tricky.

VA(s) 661, which is a dirt road, turns 90 degrees to the right at a row of mailboxes. Do *not* follow the turn, but instead go straight ahead onto a small unmarked country lane. This gradually narrows to a two-track overhung with small trees, leading downward toward the streambed. It sounds worse than it is and does not require a four-wheel-drive vehicle when dry, although the last couple of hundred yards require bouncing from rock to rock. It dead-ends at streamside, next to the remains of a swinging bridge, and this is still public roadway with parking no problem as long as you do not block access to the summer cabins to the right and left. This was once a ford, but one look at the opposite bank affirms that Hurricane Hugo has barricaded the road with an impossible maze of blowdowns. Fishing is excellent both up- and downstream from the former ford.

The key to gaining access to Laurel Fork is to explore, explore, explore, as it does not pass through any public land. The route described above leads to a relatively private stretch of stream, but some nosing about will undoubtedly lead to equally good access.

Laurel Fork is a beautiful stream, and it's large as Virginia trout waters go, averaging 75 feet across, downstream from the village of Laurel Fork. Its abundant flow comes from frequent feeder streams, cooling the water in summer. It has stretches of relatively slow rapids, most of which are deep enough to hold trout well. It's not the sort of mountain stream that has falls with deep holes beneath but rather follows a gentle gradient with riffles followed by flat rapids.

The stocked rainbows are hefty fish, running a foot or larger in length with deep, heavy bodies. There is evidence of spawning activity, boding well for the holdover population. Fish have been observed in late autumn feeding upon hoppers and unidentified large-winged terrestrials. The Muddler Minnow was effective dropped into the rapids and allowed to drift into backwater pools.

A few miles away is Burk's Fork, prominently visible from the roads leading to Laurel Fork and similar to that stream. Burk's Fork is not listed separately in this book because all access appears to be from the shoulder of paved roadway, except where the land is heavily posted. There may be convenient public access somewhere, but it is not readily apparent.

There are signs of heavy fishing on Laurel Fork at the end of the more hidden access roads, as might be expected, since there are so few of them. On the other hand, there are long stretches of stream along the paved county roads, such as VA(s) 630. The stream is somewhat abused here, with dumping and an occasional submerged tire. One would do well to move upstream from the roads and explore the more obscure stretches of Laurel Fork.

Of course, there are no barely touched trout streams in the eastern United States, although the closest you can get to them is in Virginia's Appalachians. No matter how far upstream you wade Laurel Fork, the tips of overhanging rhododendron limbs have been stripped bare of leaves, mementos of anglers grabbing for stability while navigating occasional slippery rock ledges. Fortunately, there are stretches of gravel, making for less demanding wading, and even among the ledges strips of gravel provide a foothold for dunk-free casting.

LITTLE STONY CREEK

Stream Type Freestone

Maps USGS Eggleston; DeLorme 41

Access From I-81 take exit 118 at Christiansburg to Bypass US 460 west. Follow Bypass US 460 and US 460 through the town of Pembroke, where a national forest sign indicates the CASCADES (not to be confused with the Cascades at the Homestead). Turn right here onto VA(s) 623, which takes you to a parking area just below the regulated fishing. Don't be confused by other Little Stony Creeks, as there are many duplications of names in Virginia. These were isolated settlements at the time the streams were christened, and the surveyors just wrote on their maps any name that seemed to fit the milieu.

The Little Stony is one of those good news–bad news streams that portend the future of trout fishing in the state of Virginia. Most of the news is good. This is a regulated stream, single-hook artificial lures only. It is not stocked but manages to maintain a good population of both rainbow and brook trout.

In the early 1940s the Little Stony was stocked with rainbows. The stocking "took," and its descendants are still around. One piece of good news is that the brook trout have managed to coexist with their more aggressive rainbow neighbors, which does not always happen. The Little Stony is also lucky enough to have been chosen by Trout Unlimited for its brand of enlightened attention.

So what's the bad news? Perhaps the worst of it is apathy—meaning there are "power bait" anglers who occasionally take advantage of the Little Stony's fragile ecology. Probably the worst news is that there aren't more regulated Little Stonys around the state. We hope that will change.

If someone had said, "We're going to design the model Appalachian trout stream. First of all, it must be crystal clear and pure, with nothing around it but national forest. Second, it must have cascades with deep green holes below. Third, it must be scenic, with hemlocks, laurels, wildflowers, and a few mossy boulders scattered around. And fourth, there must be a good variety of aquatic insects, particularly caddis flies and midges, but with a good cross section of mayflies," the result would have been the Little Stony.

As you cross the Little Stony's lower footbridge, the first thing that strikes your eye is a pod of rainbows lying beneath the rippled surface. Backlit with an amber light from somewhere, the underwater rock ledges frame the 12- to 14-inch fish. Most of the Trout Unlimited people who come here bypass these showcase fish and head upstream.

As one TU member said, "I start out on the Little Stony by just sitting

Harry Steeves is about to land a native brookie on his favorite stream, Little Stony.

down in the water, because it's certainly going to happen to me anyway."
Maybe an exaggeration, but there's no doubt about the slickness of these
rocks; when you add in the heavy current dropping down the mountainside,
a wading staff can be a friend indeed. Contrary to the usual pattern, the holes
get deeper and wider as you fish upstream, probably because the steeper gradient there causes the water to churn away more of the streambed.

There are walking trails on both banks of the stream, placed there by the
Jefferson National Forest Commission, which maintains them regularly.
Many people come just to walk the trail to the cascades, where another footbridge crosses. Above the cascades there is some trout activity, but you soon
hit private land. The rainbows take caddis flies and light mayfly ties but will
also slam a floating black ant cast into the rapids. There's abundant overhanging laurel, rhododendron, and hemlock, so be prepared for much
patient untangling and unhooking from the vegetation.

This is challenging terrain that calls for an experienced fly-angler to take
full advantage of its charms. It's not the sort of stream to which you would
take novices for their first fly-casting lessons. Casts may be short, with a
quick retrieve to keep the line from bellying. This rapid casting pattern, combined with maintaining your footing in slippery-rock rapids, makes the Little
Stony a physically demanding day's workout. But with the right fly patterns
and a little skill, you'll catch decent-sized fish here for a stream this small. So
you take a pratfall or two in the icy water—it's more than well worth it!

POTTS CREEK (JAMES RIVER DRAINAGE)

Stream Type Limestone

Maps USGS Potts Creek; DeLorme 40, 52

Access Take US 311 from exit 140 off I-81 at Salem and go north to Paint Bank. From the state trout hatchery, proceed to the bottom of the mountain and take VA(s) 18 to the right, which is north. Continue to the Steel Bridge Campground, maintained by the U.S. Forest Service.

A large stream by Virginia mountain standards, Potts Creek has an abundance of terrestrials and some productive mayfly hatches, green drakes and sulphur duns in particular. From the steel bridge downstream this is considered mainly a bass fishery, although some large trout hang at the junctions of small feeder streams, of which there are many. When there is a mayfly hatch below the Steel Bridge Campground, casting to a rise will almost invariably produce a rock bass or a feisty smallmouth. The prime trout water is upstream from the campground, with deep holes and some of the slickest rocks you'll find. At the steel bridge there is a slate bottom, with knife edges that give good traction but are unkind to the hands if you should fall. Above and below this slate area is a reddish Catawba stone bottom with a surface resembling glass.

These trout are large, and they're wily in June from the heavy fishing pressure they received early in the season. The waters tend to warm up later in the summer, so it's best to visit Potts Creek before the July heat sets in. Traveling the bank is not recommended, as there is a proliferation of greenbrier, designed to cause misery, grabbing landing nets or tearing new buttonholes in designer clothes. It's best to stay with the streambed.

This stream is stocked regularly and is one of the more productive Virginia fisheries. An article in the Roanoke newspaper tells of a local fisherman taking 112 trout in a day from one elongated rock-bed pool. The story continues that these were freshly stocked fish, taken by jigging 2-inch minnows. Using this method, the gentleman caught a total of 734 trout in the spring of 1990. That's the downside of the story. The upside is that he is not a keeper, and all fish were returned to Potts Creek mainly unharmed. The other upbeat note is that there are plenty of trout, some of them uncommonly large, in this stream. Using a weighted Muddler Minnow, the fly-angler can replicate this number-cruncher's experience.

SINKING CREEK

Stream Type Spring creek

Maps USGS Newport; DeLorme 41

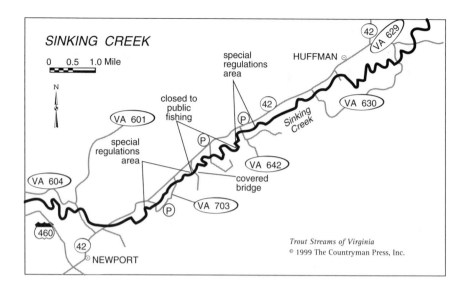

Special Regulations Single-hook, fly-fishing only. Creel limit, two fish per day, 16 inches or longer. All fish less than 16 inches must be returned immediately to the water unharmed, and possession of trout less than 16 inches long while fishing this stream is illegal. No bait may be in possession in this regulated area. Fishing is permitted year-round. No camping or fires are allowed. Access to the stream is from designated parking areas and fence crossings only. Written permission is required to fish. Permits may be obtained at the True Value store in Newport or Twin Oaks store on VA 42 near Simmonsvillle.

Access At Newport, turn east off US 460 onto VA 42 for 2 miles. Turn right on VA(s) 703 across a low-water concrete bridge. The main parking area is just to the left.

When you stand beside VA 42, looking down at the covered bridge and then the sweep of mountain and pastureland that is the Sinking Creek Valley, you experience the exhilaration of starting a day's fly-fishing. A closer look at the stream reveals an almost western look. It's a large stream by Blue Ridge standards, averaging 50 feet across on some stretches. Below the bridge are several large boulders, adding to the Colorado illusion. The stream drops gradually down to the town of Newport, then crosses under US 460. Something remarkable happens on this last stretch. The flow becomes sparser and sparser. Then, finally, in a meadow just above the New River, Sinking Creek lives up to its name and quietly disappears.

One 3.5-mile stretch from VA(s) 642 to VA(s) 703 has become a model of Virginia trout management. In 1990 a landowner named Larry Reynolds,

In early spring, the rapids on Sinking Creek show the powerful flow of the stream.

who owned the majority of streamside property in the valley, approached the state game and fish commission and asked that his part of the stream be declared a bass fishery. The idea was to furnish recreation for local children.

The responsible official, Joe Williams, studied the trout history here. It seems that for years Sinking Creek was a put-and-take stream, which led to friction with the landowners due to trash and tearing up of fences. It was posted and closed to fishing. But when active, Sinking Creek produced holdover trout of 20 or even 24 inches. This started Joe Williams thinking, and he went down to the valley and met with landowners. "Look," he said. "There's the potential to develop some big trout here—wild trout, eventually. If you're interested, we'll make this into a trout fishery of some sort."

The landowners agreed, and one enthusiastic fly-fishing resident, Miller Williams, became the spokesman for the program. His enthusiasm, coming from one whose family's farming of the Sinking Creek Valley dated into antebellum times, is what allowed the trout-management program to succeed. Joe Williams brought in Trout Unlimited members, who met with Miller Williams and the landowners to map out strategy. Some of the private landowners, not the TU or state people, urged that fly-fishing-only be declared. Everyone agreed, and in July of 1990, 2,000 sizable rainbows and browns were stocked. They had to be large; the whopping-big smallmouth and rock bass that owned the stream would make a quick lunch of fingerling trout.

In 1991 the state returned and stocked well over 5,000 more fish. But at the end of the summer of 1991, they sampled the population and were puzzled. They could find only a few trout. It seemed the water had warmed too much and the fish had moved to cooler spots. That theory was borne out by some anglers' catching impressively mature fish from that original stocking. At this writing, some of those grandfather fish can still be spotted, but catching them is another proposition. They may have been hooked 9 or 10 times during their lifetime, and they have an eye for artificials.

Water temperature is still a problem. Joe Williams reported testing just above the low-water bridge in late August and finding a temperature of 72 degrees. This was alarming, until he moved below the bridge, less than 100 feet away, and found the water to be in the low 50s. A small tributary empties in at that point and is typical of the spring branches and streambed springs that sustain trout during warm weather.

Sinking Creek is one of the very few spring creeks in Virginia, Mossy Creek being another example. The difference between the two streams is the lack of in-stream vegetation in Sinking Creek to provide top cover for trout. Cover log projects are under way to make up for the lack. There is no bedrock to speak of, and the bottom is mostly gravel, making for easy wading. Frequent redds may be spotted in the clear water, in plenty of time to wade around them.

In the early spring, nymphs are most effective on Sinking Creek. Prolific hatches of sulphur duns have been observed, and matching them can even catch big long-term resident browns off guard. There is a good minnow population, and streamers with a touch of red plus the old reliable Muddler Minnows work well. The more mature rainbows and browns are reported to feed almost exclusively on minnows.

The fly-fishing-only area is divided into three stretches. It's possible to fish all 3.5 miles in a day, but any one of them will provide a day's concentrated, careful pleasure. There are three designated parking areas. The upstream one is off the shoulder of the road and is marked with a sign on the stream side of VA 42.

The center section, overlooking the covered bridge, uses a paved area across VA 42 from a turnstile. Incidentally, TU has installed turnstiles all along the stream wherever there is a fence to be crossed.

The downstream parking area is reached by crossing the low-water bridge at the end of VA(s) 703 and turning left. Continuing straight will put you on a private drive, where the homeowner has been promised no intruders. The regulated area continues downstream from the low-water bridge just short of a quarter of a mile. From the road in you can look downstream and see the end marker on a cable across the stream.

SNAKE CREEK

Stream Type Freestone

Maps USGS Fancy Gap; DeLorme 25

Access Turn east off I-77 at Hillsville onto VA 58. At Red Hill turn right onto VA(s) 674. Then turn left on VA(s) 922, which follows the special-regulations section of Snake Creek.

Here's an angling enigma. This stream has been described in a state publication as having a fair population of native brook trout plus a holdover of stocked fish. And yet a look at the Snake along VA(s) 922 reveals a largely silted bottom—the stream is dammed by beavers at several points—and little evidence of trout. There is a bounty of insect life over the stream, and yet no surface feeding. The beavers have worked this stream so industriously that there are even partly gnawed trees wrapped in fence wire to protect them from further incising. Beaver damming can help the trout habitat of some fisheries, but the property along Snake Creek is so heavily grazed that these dams only cause the silt to accumulate even more alarmingly.

The Big Snake is around 18 feet wide in the special-regulations areas, with a good flow of water, following a slight gradient downstream. There are no plunge pools or rapids of any significance. It is stocked periodically with fish 8 to 10 inches in length.

With a lot of cooperation from landowners and intensive management by the Virginia Department of Game and Inland Fisheries, Snake Creek has the potential of becoming a four-star brown trout fishery. It's far from being there at this time, however, and may take years to develop fully.

STEWART'S CREEK

Stream Type Freestone

Maps USGS Lambsburg; DeLorme 24

Access Take I-77 south past Hillsville and across the Blue Ridge Parkway. Exit on VA(s) 620 to the west through Lambsburg, where you turn left onto

Steve Hiner works Stewart's Creek one 47-degree December morning.

VA(s) 696. After a short distance, turn right onto VA(s) 795, which leads into the Stewart's Creek Wildlife Management Area. The road dead-ends beside the stream in a parking area.

Stewart's Creek is still a heavily pressured stream, though it has been converted to a catch-and-release trout fishery. Nevertheless, it is holding its own as a prolific stream. One angler counted over 100 strikes in a day, mostly small fish, and mostly missed due to early-season rustiness. It's a high-gradient freestone stream with a dense riparian canopy, mostly rhododendron. Surrounded by over 1,000 acres of the Stewart's Creek Wildlife Management Area owned by the state, it flows for around 4.5 miles in Virginia, including the North and South Forks. It drains, ultimately, into North Carolina's Yadkin River, but is close enough to the New River Drainage area to warrant inclusion in this chapter.

The state of Virginia purchased this property in 1987 just in time to save Stewart's Creek from degradation due to poor logging practices. The erosion has been checked by stabilizing exposed soil through some pretty imaginative measures. What were once raw banks are covered with attractive greenery, and the waters are sparkling clear.

The lower stretch is good for a fair number of small, scrappy brook trout, which may be easily seen darting over the gravel-and-stone bottom.

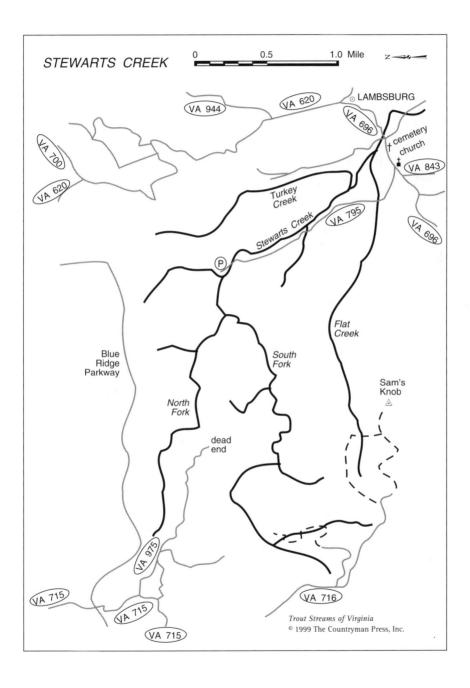

STEWARTS CREEK

0   0.5   1.0 Mile   N

VA 944   VA 620   ⊙ LAMBSBURG

VA 696

VA 700

VA 620

Turkey
Creek

Stewarts Creek   VA 795

† cemetery
church
VA 843

VA 696

P

Flat
Creek

Blue
Ridge
Parkway

South
Fork

Sam's
Knob
⚠

North
Fork

dead
end

VA 975

VA 715

VA 716

VA 715

Trout Streams of Virginia
© 1999 The Countryman Press, Inc.

VA 715

Farther upstream the gradient becomes much steeper, with plunge pools around every 50 feet, still averaging 10 feet in width. The brookies are larger here, and as plentiful as one would think in a catch-and-release environment where only single-hook artificial lures are permitted.

The farther up the mountain you go, the steeper and more interesting Stewart's gets. From 100 feet up on the vertical slope, you can occasionally spot a sizable trout. The trick then is to lower yourself down the bank slowly and carefully enough not to scare him, then drop your Adams number 16 upstream in front of his nose. If he gulps it, you are then dazzled by brilliant scarlet flashes as he porpoises around the pool.

In addition to using attractor flies such as the Adams, you may find it possible to match an assortment of mayfly hatches rising throughout the year. Even in mid-December some olive quill nymphs and mature stoneflies are in evidence, along with the usual midges inevitably appearing around midday.

> **Author's Note** *My normally reliable minnow imitations, such as a weighted Muddler, appeared to hold no attraction for the Stewart's feeders on a day when the water temperature measured 47 degrees at 11 AM. On this mid-December day the ambient temperature was above 60 degrees, so the water warmed up even more later in the afternoon. There are no absolutes on these native trout streams, and a premeditated cookbook approach simply doesn't work. But that's what keeps it interesting.*

On the South Fork, there is a last upper stretch of source water that leads almost vertically up the north slope of Sam's Knob. More demanding for the angler than the lower stretches, it may be the last habitat for generations of native trout that escaped the past century's logging operations. A more civilized route to this upper stretch heads down from above, leading off the Blue Ridge Parkway onto VA(s) 715. Then take a left onto VA(s) 975, at the STEWART'S CREEK WILDLIFE MANAGEMENT AREA sign. This leads in slightly over a mile to a dead end at the North Fork.

7 | Mount Rogers National Recreation Area

Driving out VA 58 toward the Whitetop Laurel, a newcomer may try to catch a glimpse of Mount Rogers, Virginia's highest at 5,729 feet. But there are no Wyoming Rockies here, thrusting above the horizon. These are old mountains, and Rogers is a round-shouldered giant hidden behind a rampart of wooded foothills. To the southwest is Whitetop Mountain, 5,540 feet, and Pine Mountain, 5,526 feet, all within the 154,000-acre Mount Rogers Recreation Area, most of which is included in the Jefferson National Forest.

The three wilderness areas here are Lewis Fork, 5,730 acres; Little Dry Run, 3,400 acres; and Little Wilson Creek, 3,855 acres—adjacent to Grayson Highlands State Park. Little Wilson is the one of most interest to anglers, with a native trout fishery that wanders between alpine meadows down to Wilson Creek.

This part of the state, sometimes called the Virginia Highlands, is a many-faceted gem. If you like trout fishing amid cascades of purple rhododendron or banks of pink and white laurel, this is the place to come in April. You run the risk of having your eye distracted from your floating Adams by the dazzling scene around every bend in the stream.

BIG TUMBLING CREEK

Stream Type Freestone

Maps USGS Saltville; DeLorme 22

Special Regulations Big Tumbling is fee-fishing water: a daily permit costing $3.50 is required in addition to a Virginia fishing license. The permit can be obtained at the refreshment area; special trout license not required. The water is closed to fishing each evening at specified times depending on the hour of sunset; anglers are advised to confirm the closing time, for there is a $40 fine for fishing when the stream is closed.

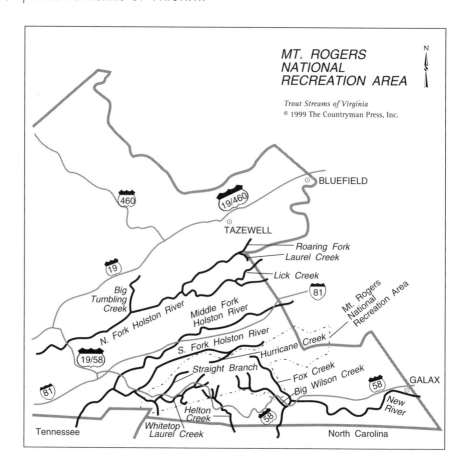

Access From I-81 take exit 35, following VA 107 through Chilhowie north to Saltville. Turn left on VA 91 at Saltville, then, within 0.5 mile, right on VA(s) 634 to Allison's Gap, left on VA(s) 613, and right on VA(s) 747. Look for signs reading CLINCH MOUNTAIN WILDLIFE MANAGEMENT AREA.

What strikes you most when you enter the Big Tumbling Gorge is the perpetual twilight, even at midmorning on a July day. It's cool, dim, and steep, with the stream living up to its name by rolling noisily from the top of Clinch Mountain. How steep? Well, steep enough that the fish-management people stock the stream by cable, lowering containers of fish on pulleys into pools at the foot of stair-step rapids. Stocking takes place every day except Sunday. At the headwaters, on the mountaintop, Laurel Bed Lake is stocked in November with as many as 8,000 brook trout.

Sure, this is a fee-fishing stream, but angling here is anything but easy. Thigh muscles will get a workout, and much of your travel time may be spent clinging to branches hanging over the steep banks. Because of the dim light imposed by overhanging bowers of hemlock and oak, light-colored dry flies work well: a Light Cahill number 12 or a White Moth, for example. Muddler Minnow number 12s with metallic and red enhancement are recommended in deep pools beneath falls and rapids. These are sizable and healthy fish, many of them holdovers, and they show a lot of fight in the relatively small Big Tumbling pools.

BIG WILSON CREEK

Stream Type Freestone

Maps USGS Troutdale; DeLorme 23

Access From I-81, take exit 45 onto VA 16 south to Volney. Proceed to the intersection and take VA 58 west. Where Wilson Creek crosses under a bridge, take VA(s) 817, a dirt road that traces the Big Wilson to its source.

Big Wilson is typical of rhododendron-lined streams in the Virginia Highlands area. From the road, its waters seem lost at times in the maze of trailer-sized boulders. These give the angler a screen for approaching pools unseen and provide pockets for trout protection. Walking down to streamside, you see a healthy small-stone-and-pebble bottom, abundant water from mountain-spring branches, and stair steps of falls and pools at frequent intervals. Almost every pool harbors at least one small holdover rainbow well into winter.

Higher on the mountainside, the stream, appropriately labeled Big Wilson down to the village called Mouth of Wilson, is just plain Wilson Creek. As you proceed upstream, the state stocking signs run out, along with the beaten paths and litter. As the stream narrows, it becomes classic native trout water. Above two summer cabins the road becomes more of a series of semilevel boulder tops, requiring a four-wheel drive—difficult access but worth it. There is now a special-regulations section up there: Single-hook artificial lures only, and all fish under 9 inches are to be returned.

Stoneflies are an important item in the diet of Big Wilson trout, as in other streams around the Mount Rogers area. The five key stonefly species provide both spring and winter hatches. A genus of giant stonefly, *Pteronarcys,* is common here, and may be imitated in its nymph stage with a Giant Black Stone nymph pattern, which makes a hefty mouthful. For more picky eaters, the little yellow stonefly is particularly prevalent in these freestone headwaters from May to July. Among other mayflies, green drakes emerge abundantly in May here and in the other Mount Rogers streams.

The overhanging vegetation makes terrestrials a consideration as well. There are times when only beetles and ants are taken near the Wilson's banks, while midstream trout are feeding on some form of aquatic insects.

FOX CREEK

Stream Type Freestone

Maps USGS Troutdale; DeLorme 23

Access From I-81 take exit 45 onto VA 16 south and continue to Troutdale. Turn west (right) there onto VA(s) 603 to Fairwood, center of the Fox Creek Restoration Area.

Fox Creek is one of those on-again, off-again conservation stories all too familiar to those who like to see trout restored to a classic stream. At the beginning of this century, Grayson County's Fairwood Valley was a showplace of all the best of the Virginia Highlands. Virgin spruce and hemlock completed their life cycles as they had for thousands of years, and Fox Creek brimmed with brook trout.

The industrial revolution in Grayson County took the form of Shay locomotives chuffing up the mountainsides and carrying away the heritage of the "Deep Woods," as Virginia was once called. Even with muscle and crosscut saws, it only took a few years to level the forest, leaving the land ravaged and the soil unprotected. Cattle cropped what little streamside vegetation remained, topsoil washed away, and fires ran through the dry slash left by loggers. Nevertheless, in spite of average water temperatures around 78 degrees, the maximum survival limit of rainbow trout, a few hardy fish remained. The brookies long ago retreated upstream to Lewis Fork, a small feeder at the headwaters. Then in the early 1980s the Virginia Department of Game and Inland Fisheries selected Fox Creek as a model of stream rehabilitation. In 1983 the first log channel constrictors and dams were set in place. But it wasn't until 1987 that the cattle standing in Fox Creek, blissfully unaware of the damage they were causing, were barred from the stream by fences complete with turnstiles for anglers. Since then some 3,400 trout have been placed in the stream annually, with the hope that eventually wild trout will reproduce in the improved habitat.

The streamside vegetation proliferated, cutting down the "limit-out" bait-fishing crowd and leaving room for fly-anglers. The rainbow population grew steadily. Then in the fall of 1989 Hurricane Hugo struck, carrying away fences and K-dams, and fanning out the mica-laden soil back into flat stretches that heat up past trout survival limits. Since then the cooperative effort between the U.S. Forest Service and the Virginia Department of Inland Fisheries to rehabilitate the stream continues and is strongly supported by the work of individual trout fishermen. A lot of sweat and funding has gone into overcoming the abuse of Fox Creek and restoring it as a valuable coldwater fishery. It's holding rainbow trout, but the hurricane's effects will take some years to overcome.

A visit to Fox Creek is worth it—for the fishing, but also to observe trout conservation at its best. At this point the only element strongly lacking is an area restricted to artificial, single-hook lures along the most critical 1.5-mile stretch. The Fox can be fished for many miles below the regulated area, with some excellent spots worth exploring. This is mostly private land, and permission from owners should be obtained. If you fish Fox Creek, fish it gently, and remember that every rainbow you release may become a parent.

HOLSTON RIVER, SOUTH FORK

Stream Type Limestone

Maps USGS Marion; DeLorme 22, 23

Access At exit 45 from I-81 follow VA 16 north to US 11; turn left onto US 11 and after two blocks, turn left onto VA(s) 658. Follow 658 south to a left on VA(s) 657, and after a short distance another left onto VA(s) 650. Follow 650 to the Buller Fish Cultural Station, turning in at the sign there. Go upstream on a gravel road, past the fish hatchery, to a cable across the road barring vehicles.

Another access to the South Holston may be gained west of VA 16 near Sugar Grove, off VA(s) 672 right at the intersection of VA(s) 670, where a sign indicates VALLEY VIEW BAPTIST CHURCH. The first glance may be misleading, as a wooden bridge leads across the Holston into someone's front yard. The homeowner is very understanding of stream-lashers, however, and enormous rainbows can be spotted straightaway beneath the bridge. Working downstream, taking care not to damage the grass, you can often find more good-sized trout flashing bottoms-up while working nymphs and snails on the bed. Then suddenly the river is surrounded by woods, and only a dim path parallels its course. It's narrower here, resembling a true Virginia Highlands stream, and it harbors some smaller natives for a good distance downstream.

As you follow the South Holston past Buller Fish Cultural Station, it's worth a stop to take a look at the muskies raised there. Although the main product of the fishery is bass, you'll probably find at least one toothy monster 3 feet long, staring unblinkingly with crocodile eyes. These are not what you came for, though they are stocked liberally in surrounding lakes and warm-water fisheries. Getting back on your way, you drive upstream past a dam and reach a cable closing the road to vehicles. From here it's trout all the way.

From this point there are a couple of choices, one being to wade the stream above the dam—from the place where the impoundment becomes shallow enough—into a gorge with some pretty tough white water. (By the

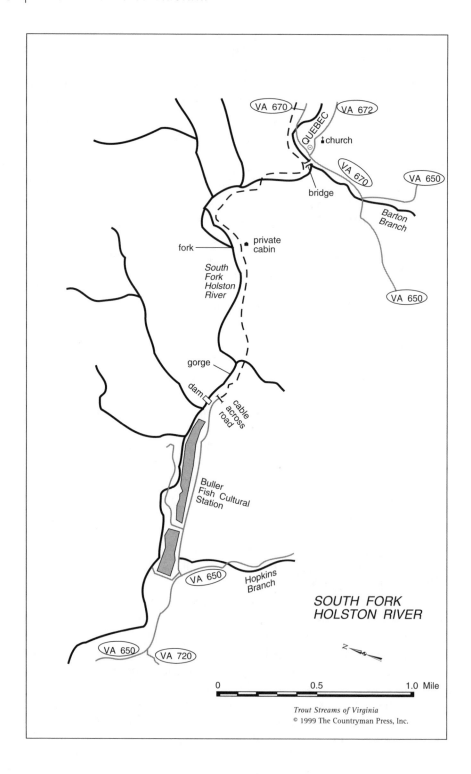

VA 670
VA 672
QUEBEC
church
VA 670
VA 650
bridge
Barton Branch
fork — private cabin
South Fork Holston River
VA 650
gorge
dam
cable across road
Buller Fish Cultural Station
VA 650
Hopkins Branch
VA 650
VA 720

SOUTH FORK HOLSTON RIVER

N

0   0.5   1.0 Mile

Trout Streams of Virginia
© 1999 The Countryman Press, Inc.

way, this is chest-wader water even during the low-water months of summer, as the Holston is well fed by mountain streams and limestone springs all along its course.) The other choice will be to shoulder your waders and hike over a mile up a fair-sized hill to where the river levels out somewhat. It's a relief to find a trout stream of this width in the Virginia Highlands, and backcasting is relatively free of snags. Before starting your uphill hike, casting from the bank into the deep water above the dam will attract some darting rainbows, but these fish have seen a dry fly before and invariably turn away at the last second.

At the upper level there are long stretches of still water over deep pockets among the rocks. Trout may be seen popping flies softly from the surface of the relatively quiet water. Occasional hatches of green drakes, hendricksons, light cahills, and stoneflies occur, with the dictates of match-the-hatch determining which to tie on, because of the variety of flies found here. In the rapids a wet Olive Dun or Coachman may be preferable, with an occasional big brown going after a Woolly Bugger.

Allow a day to explore the Holston's South Fork, as each bend presents a new set of challenges—casting approaches and varied insect life—to be analyzed. At the mountaintop is a large private cabin just below a fork in the river. The water runs across a stream-wide slate ledge and dumps into a foaming trough of dark green water just beneath the fork. This spot alone is worth an hour of fishing. Above the fork there is no stocking and few native brookies and rainbows. For the hardier fisherman who still hasn't had enough of this seductive river, there's plenty of smaller water upstream. Downstream is some put-and-take water, with citation holdover browns and some big rainbows.

Much of the stream is special regulations—single-hook artificial lures only, all fish under 9 inches to be released—and the hatchery section is catch-and-release.

HURRICANE CREEK

Stream Type Freestone

Maps USGS Whitetop Mountain; DeLorme 23

Access From I-81 take exit 45 south on US 16 into the Mount Rogers National Recreation Area. A worthwhile stop is the area headquarters, where a detailed map may be obtained, along with answers to any questions. Proceed south on 16 to a sign indicating a right turn onto VA(s) 650 leading to the HURRICANE CAMPGROUND. From here it's all downhill, with the road rimming hundred-foot drop-offs worthy of the Rockies, but with more trees to catch you. Finally you reach bottom and cross the Hurricane on a bridge into the campground.

The author floats a midge under a fallen tree on a Mount Rogers stream.

The Virginia Highlands is a specific region in the state's southwest pan-handle wedged between Tennessee and Kentucky. Mount Rogers, the state's highest mountain, is located here, along with ridges almost equaling its height. The wealth of the area is in its waters, which roll exuberantly from the mountaintops in some locations and quietly trickle through the gorges thousands of feet below in others. The Hurricane is one example of those quiet, low-lying streams of the Highlands.

Although hundreds of feet below the brow of Seng Mountain, this little stream has an active brook trout life of its own, with small rapids and holes alternating. By the way, *seng* is the local vernacular for ginseng, whose root is renowned for medicinal and aphrodisiac qualities and which still brings income to those mountain people hardy enough to break through the under-brush where there are no paths. Occasionally during midcast you may be overrun by a wild-eyed, lean bunch of people loping through the woods. These are the seng gatherers, usually active in early fall when the special brilliant yellow of the ginseng plant is unmistakable from hundreds of yards away. During June the woods are slashed with a similar bold color, the light yellow to deep orange of wild azalea blossoms.

Hurricane Creek, also called Hurricane Branch, is small enough to be fished without benefit of waders. Red and black ants are effective, as are olive nymphs cast up into the rapids and allowed to cascade over into holed-out rocks. Don't expect too much mayfly action, as the small, restless Hurricane is not ideal for their hatches.

LAUREL CREEK

Stream Type Freestone

Maps USGS Hutchinson's Rock; DeLorme 39

Access This and the next stream can be reached by the same route: Leave I-81 at exit 45 on VA 16 and go north. Follow VA 16 north past Hungry Mother State Park and across Walker and Brushy Mountains. Then just over the crest of Clinch Mountain, behind a cut bank, there's a dirt road leading down the mountain to the right. There is no marking and no route sign, but this is FR 222. Look down the mountainside for a dirt road snaking its way to the east. If you continue down Clinch Mountain on VA 16 to Thompson Valley, you've missed it, but fortunately the turnoff is much more visible as you return southbound. A stop at Monk's Store is a good idea, as the proprietor has fished the local waters for trout for many years and is willing to share his experience, as well as directions.

FR 222 is a well-traveled dirt-and-gravel roadway, with hunting cabins scattered in the Jefferson National Forest land. You will cross a wooden bridge spanning Laurel Creek, with plenty of parking space at streamside.

The first stream encountered on FR 222 in Tazewell County is Laurel Creek, crossed there by a wooden bridge. There is a stocking sign posted, and a well-used clearing. From the bridge upstream, Laurel Creek departs from the road up onto the side of Clinch Mountain. It becomes a native trout fishery along the way, well worth the effort of wading and climbing upstream.

Downstream there is a very rough and rutted road following Laurel Creek, eventually joining up with VA(s) 601. The downstream section is much more conveniently reached by turning east off VA 16 in the Freestone Valley and following VA(s) 601 up the Laurel. Despite its relatively small size, this stream produces some citation-length rainbows and brookies. Its frequent rapids and falls will quickly dunk a dry fly, making streamers and Muddler Minnows more practical. Use a quick wrist on your retrieve.

LICK CREEK

Stream Type Freestone

Maps USGS Hutchinson's Rock; DeLorme 39

Access Proceed as for Laurel Creek, on page 151. Approximately 7 miles down FR 222, past Laurel Creek, you begin seeing good trout water on Lick Creek to the left of the road. Some exploring along the bank, where the stream departs from the road, reveals excellent fishing.

A successful local trout fisherman puts Lick Creek high on his list, second only to the South Holston. According to him, plenty of trout can be caught on this modest stream even in late fall, and not necessarily at painfully early morning hours. He uses small weighted Blackflies tied wet and whatever terrestrials are crawling on a given day.

> **Author's Note** *Although I have had very little experience fishing this stream, one incident stands out. I was walking the bank idly scanning its waters when suddenly I realized what I was looking at was a 14- or 15-inch rainbow fanning his tail in the sunlight. Because of his size, unusual in these waters, I rushed back to my vehicle for my fly-rod. Returning carefully to the hole, I followed all the correct procedures, crouching low, moving slowly, and inching to within casting distance. It was a flat area, with no natural cover, and as I raised my WondeRod for a backcast, the fish vanished. I just caught a glimpse of him streaking under the submerged roots of an oak tree, where he faded into a cave he had staked out there.*
>
> *I tried everything, drifting an assortment of flies, ants, and minnow replicas before his hiding place. But no amount of tweaking, darting, drifting, or dangling would bring him out of his sulk.*

STRAIGHT BRANCH

Stream Type Freestone

Maps USGS Konnarock; DeLorme 22

Access From I-81 take exit 45 on VA 16 south to US 58 west. Heading west from Konnarock to Damascus on 58, take a right at the sign reading BEARTREE CAMPGROUND. Beartree Lake is a stocked trout fishery, with prescribed swimming areas along with a sand beach.

Straight Branch is another of the small Virginia native trout streams that require special skills. It is backed up by a dam into Beartree Lake, which is stocked with trout. Above and below the lake this is a laurel-and-rhododendron-covered fishery, with the water somewhat snuff-colored by the cedar roots surrounding it. There are stocked brook trout here, but the problem is getting a fly into the pools where they live. The interlacing network of branches arches over impoundments caused by occasional hemlock or cedar tree trunks that have been felled by nature or the Game and Inland Fisheries people.

These small pools abound with life, including several varieties of minnows and insects falling from the surrounding vegetation. It's not the sort of stream conducive to classic mayfly hatches, but rainbow trout can comfortably complete their life cycles on terrestrials and underwater life-forms. There's little casting to be done, because of the near impossibility of snaking

The author angles on the Whitetop Laurel.

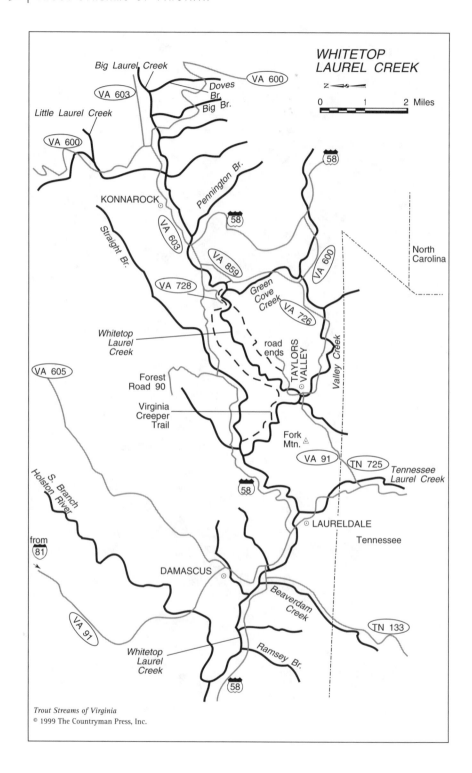

WHITETOP
LAUREL CREEK

N

0   1   2 Miles

Big Laurel Creek

Doves Br.

Big Br.

VA 600

VA 603

Little Laurel Creek

VA 600

Pennington Br.

58

KONNAROCK

VA 603

58

Straight Br.

VA 859

North Carolina

VA 600

VA 728

Green Cove Creek

VA 726

Whitetop Laurel Creek

road ends

TAYLORS VALLEY

Valley Creek

VA 605

Forest Road 90

Virginia Creeper Trail

Fork Mtn.

VA 91

TN 725

Tennessee Laurel Creek

S. Branch Holston River

58

LAURELDALE

Tennessee

from 81

DAMASCUS

Beaverdam Creek

TN 133

VA 91

Whitetop Laurel Creek

Ramsey Br.

58

Trout Streams of Virginia
© 1999 The Countryman Press, Inc.

a fly between the heavy undergrowth, and consequently the Straight is not a put-and-take stream.

Below Beartree, Straight Branch widens slightly, even though it's less than 6 feet across in most places. The lower stretch is stocked, but it's not the sort of stream likely to attract hordes of opening-day fishermen. During midsummer the water is low, though still cool enough for good trout habitat. It's worth a trip to the Straight during the hot months just to walk into the hemlock tunnels and listen to the little stream's cool clicks and gurgles.

WHITETOP LAUREL

Stream Type Freestone

Maps USGS Konnarock; DeLorme 22

Access From I-81 take exit 29 south on VA 91, which brings you into downtown Damascus, Virginia. At the intersection take US 58 east for slightly over 4 miles until you reach a sign on the right displaying the silhouette of a small steam train. Turn in here and park near the U.S. Forest Service information board. Proceed on foot up the mountain on an old cinder railroad bed, which is the Virginia Creeper Trail. A series of wooden "trestles," minus rails and crossties, span the Whitetop Laurel, and fishing is best above the fourth trestle, near the top of Fork Mountain.

There is another Whitetop Laurel, or so it seems, even though it's actually the same stream, and that's the one in Taylor's Valley. This stretch is reached by taking US 58 east from Damascus and turning south on VA 91. You'll cross the line and for 2 minutes see a bit of Johnson County, Tennessee. After a mile or so take the only paved road to the left, which is Tennessee secondary road 725, looping back into Virginia. After the pavement ends there is a temptation to turn upstream on VA(s) 726, but persevere on 725 across a wooden bridge and to the left. The road ends in what appears to be someone's front yard—and in fact it is. But you may park there and walk about a quarter of a mile upstream to a wooden trestle. From there upstream is a 3-mile stretch of regulated water, fishable only with single-hook artificial lures.

The stretch below the trestle and into Taylor's Valley is not restricted, and good fishing may be had throughout its entire length. For the hardy, fishing from US 58 up the Virginia Creeper cinder trail and across the mountain into Taylor's Valley would be more than a full day. But it would take you into some wild trout fishing that would leave material for some unbeatable winter-evening reminiscing.

There is some confusion about the Whitetop Laurel's name. More traditional maps show a Whitetop Valley Creek and a Laurel Creek, which join at Taylor's Valley. Some of the newer maps now show a Whitetop Laurel.

But when you ask local residents about either tributary, they invariably reply, "Oh, you mean the Whitetop Laurel."

Whatever you call it, this is a premier trout stream. If you had time to fish only one trout water in the state of Virginia, it probably should be the Whitetop Laurel, especially now that the special-regulations section has been extended (single-hook, artificial lures only, and all fish under 9 inches must be returned). It's a magnificent display of what is best among all the Virginia Highlands streams, starting with a drop from a mountaintop, through a series of cascades, to water deep enough to dive into from a 10-foot ledge without striking bottom. Finally it skirts the backyards of Damascus, where it is possible to see a suburbanite leaning on his power mower, talking to a neighbor holding a foot-and-a-half brown trout shining like a dappled ingot in the sun. Trout is a keystone in the lives of people living around the Whitetop Laurel, and everywhere there is more than a trickle, you may be sure it contains rainbows and browns, if not brookies. One Damascus citizen is reputed to trout fish 364 days of the year, missing only Christmas—and he has been known to slip out on Christmas day if his wife turns her head.

From Damascus east to Konnarock fishing is excellent, although the real crown jewel is the Virginia Creeper Trail paralleling the stream 2 miles east of Damascus. Walking up the cinder trail, you'll find it is easy to imagine the pip-squeak engine that once labored up this mountain—to transport timber, since there is nothing else on the mountainside to justify the laying of the long-vanished track. From this trail, which is a delight to walk, small cleared paths lead off to the right into treasured fishing holes. The banks are moss-covered and easy to navigate, while the stream's gravelly bottom provides good boot traction.

The wooden railroad bridges are situated about 12 feet above the water, and if you can avoid casting a shadow, are perfect vantage points for observing the day's feeding habits. Plenty of hefty trout can be spotted from the bridges, along with an occasional calico sucker vacuuming up the stream floor. The bridge stanchions will invariably have a trout suspended beside them, ready to dart into the dark holes nearby at the first sign of an angler. In late May or early June you're likely to see fish feeding on a green drake hatch. Other good bets are hair-wing Royal Wulffs and Light Cahills.

Once the early-season pressure is off, mayfly hatches begin to hit the Whitetop Laurel, especially light cahill, sulphur dun, green drake, and ginger quill. There are lulls in the hatches, sometimes for months, due to a combination of temperatures and storm patterns. A good all-around attractor fly is an Adams number 16, which will bring a rise even if there is no surface feeding. Toward dark, a sizable White Moth will inevitably bring up fish until it's too dark to see the water. When there seems to be no possibility of rises, an Olive Caddis Pupa number 14 works well.

8 | Parkway Trout

The Blue Ridge Parkway meanders down the crest of the Blue Ridge, from the Shenandoah Park to the Great Smoky Mountains. Both of those eastern national parks offer legendary trout fishing, but fly-anglers tend to keep their rods cased during that 469-mile drive down the scenic highway that links them. Not many of these park-hoppers realize that beneath the hardwood forests seen from the parkway overlooks is a delicate tracery of mountain trout waters.

Most of these waters don't deserve to be called streams. They are springs, rills, branches, drafts, runs, or perhaps just wet spots beneath the leaves promising wild trout habitat somewhere down the slope. Some are unnamed, while others are thin blue lines on the map bearing the name of stocked streams far below in the valleys. But these tiny waters are not stocked streams—far from it. If you're lucky, they lead to stone bowls holding five or six native trout. Perhaps they are only 5 inches long, but occasionally lurking beneath a tiny waterfall will be a 12-inch patriarch, locked into his bathtub-sized domain. There may be only one trout in a pool. And sometimes there are only minnows, with no shadow of a brookie anywhere in sight.

Author's Note *I first became aware of parkway trout when talking to a ranger back in 1992. It seems that the rangers had caught a poacher under the brow of Headforemost Mountain with a plastic 5-gallon bucket containing 55 brook trout. When asked why he had captured little 3- and 4-inch trout, he glowered at them, still smarting from the size of the federal fine he had earned. Finally he replied, "Pickle 'em."*

There immediately flashed through my mind a vision of that poacher strapped to a couple of fence rails, being lowered up to his chin into a hogshead filled with pickling brine. There he would remain until some of the more sensitive areas of his anatomy were tingling smartly. Sadly, many streams I have bushwhacked into, with no sign of a trail about, will have the ominous fire ring beside the most fishable hole. The dreary conclusion is that some unprintable louts have been there, seining out every single native trout and ensuring that no breeding stock are left.

The happier side of that story came out when I asked Ranger Pete what effect that 55-count poaching would have on the stream. "That little run is so full of natives that it won't even make a dent in the population," was his answer.

Each time I hook one of these little holdovers from the last ice age, I recall that incident. It makes me just a bit more careful when I'm unhooking and returning it to its limited realm.

In the second half of this chapter I describe four streams, as a sampler of what the Blue Ridge Parkway has to offer. For the most part, these are streams I can drive to quickly from my house and fish for a couple of hours. That's as long as it takes to cover a typical small parkway stream. There are many others like these four, which represent a fair cross section of the different types of streams along the parkway. I hope this chapter will encourage you to explore many other streams in the area. A number of similar streams are described in chapter 2; they are in the Shenandoah National Park area, where the Skyline Drive joins the Blue Ridge Parkway near Waynesboro.

When going after parkway trout, it's a good idea to forget all the conventional rules of fly-casting. Don't always look for the trail, because there may not be one, except where a meandering family of deer have left a faint trace. Don't look down the mountain for a reflection off the stream, because it's hidden under the rhododendron and laurel. Trust to DeLorme, and drop off from the overlook down a swoop of mountainside that looks like a luge run across slippery leaves. The temptation is to just set your heels in front of you and slide. But the brambles and heaps of stone make that impractical.

As for equipment, a 6-foot graphite 1-ounce wand works well. The leader should not exceed the rod's length, and a line one size larger than rod spec is recommended. Forget any idea of a backcast, as you'll be standing on a slippery hummock of hemlock root, surrounded by fly-hungry underbrush. If you're lucky, a roll cast will be possible. Without another soul in sight, you can even shatter the sacred upstream casting rule and let your nymph drift with the current down into an unseen trout hideout under the bank. No one will ever know. And you might get a tug that breaks off your 7X tippet and leaves you wondering what sort of troll was hidden there.

The food supply in these little headwaters is slim, and almost any attractor fly will work, although red and black ants are a good bet during warm weather. In any season, a small black nymph, such as a Prince, will

Fishing from the bank is preferred on tiny parkway streams.

get a rise from below the moss. Turning over stones will often produce similar nondescript black aquatic life-forms. If they're tied a little on the nubby side, don't worry, as rumpling seems to add to their effectiveness. Dry flies are a luxury, useful only if you come upon an unusual pool the size of your carport that will allow a decent float. An Adams number 18 will catch some unwary surface feeders from a flat surface such as this.

If you do see surface activity in some quiet pool, don't bet on hooking into it. These little natives are not hook-shy, but they are very much aware of any movement on the bank that resembles a predator. Their lives are constantly threatened by mink, otters, kingfishers, herons, and other such fish eaters. Any movement on the bank that causes alarm will send dark little shadows darting away, ending any possibility of catching one out of that stretch.

Wading in these little parkway streams is neither a necessity nor a wise idea, because any slight ripple will make these little finned hillbillies nervous. A pair of light rubber boots is a good thing to have in your rucksack. Ankle-high, felt-soled boots such as those from Kobuck are an excellent choice. They have the added advantage of camouflage, with the Ripplin' Waters brown pattern my personal choice. These boots are mainly for marshy areas, or trails over which the stream meanders back and forth, and only occasionally are meant for wading. But when it's a really bitter

November day, you'll do well to carry along such short wader boots or even hip waders if the stream is above average parkway size.

One well-kept secret of the parkway is the story of the roadside rainbows. Years ago, when the federal bureaucracy was a bit more relaxed, bored employees would drop rainbow fingerlings into streams paralleling the roadbed. Then, during the slow seasons, they could pull over and have a quick bit of sport. It is a mystery how many of these unofficial stockers remain, but on at least one occasion, a roadside beaver pond has held a trout large enough to break a 6X leader.

Special Regulations

With few exceptions, license requirements, seasons, and hours conform to those set elsewhere by the state of Virginia. No special trout license is required when fishing parkway waters. Creel and size limits vary only in special waters, which in Virginia are Abbott Lake and Little Stony Creek. Fishing lures may be only single-hook artificials. The possession or use of live or dead fish, amphibians, or nonpreserved fish eggs is prohibited when on or along any parkway water. Digging for natural bait on parkway land is prohibited.

MATTS CREEK

Stream Type Freestone

Maps USGS Smith Mountain Dam; DeLorme 53

Access Take the Big Island exit from the Blue Ridge Parkway between mileposts 64 and 65. Turn left and go north on US 501 for 3 miles, almost to the Snowden bridge. On the left is a parking area, with an Appalachian Trail marker. Take the trail north for approximately 2.5 miles to the Matts Creek shelter. Access is also possible from the parkway near Marble Spring shelter, but the Appalachian Trail bypasses the upstream stretch of Matts Creek. This route would involve some bushwhacking over steep terrain and is not recommended.

G etting there is half the fun," many Blue Ridge fly-anglers will agree. Getting to Matts Creek may be one-quarter of the fun, or less. There is a 2.5-mile trek upstream along the Appalachian Trail, through some scenic areas of the James River Face Wilderness. You immediately follow the top of a ridge looking down on the James River Gorge. There are occasional vertical trails to the right, presumably made by spin-fishers heading down to the power-dam impound for bass. In late November the view is unobscured and spectacular, but during the warm months it may be hidden by foliage.

For a couple of reasons, Matts Creek may be an autumn fishery. Reason number one: One Appalachian Trail through-hiker reported seeing numerous copperheads around the Matts Creek shelter. As snake recognition is an essential part of his daily routine, these probably were copperheads and not northern banded water snakes, often mistaken for their fanged cousins. By mid-October, however, all snakes have normally denned up for the winter and are no longer hazards for anglers and hikers.

Reason number two: Like most Blue Ridge Parkway streams, Matts Creek is a small headwater, susceptible to summer drought. In late autumn of 1993 there was even a November drought that reduced the fishable holes to bath-tub sized. Some knowledgeable individuals labeled Matts an unproductive native trout stream after checking it as far upstream as the Appalachian Trail shelter. Fishing above the shelter, another group landed a 14-inch brook trout, along with other smaller fish.

Because it is best in the fall, terrestrials are the preferred flies, with a Crowe Beetle attracting some juvenile brook trout. But if you're looking for the twin to that 14-incher you will probably be disappointed. On the positive side, the water is filled with aquatic life, including a healthy minnow population and a variety of nymphs.

> **Author's Note** *One year, after fishing the upper portion of Matts in mid-November, I found the shadows beginning to lengthen over the stream. Reluctantly heading back down the trail, I decided not to be caught alone in the James River Face Wilderness, so I speeded up my normal pace to a lope. Suddenly I found myself kissing the stones on the trail, with a sore left knee and ankle. A round, fist-sized stone, hidden by leaves, had rolled and rendered me instantly horizontal. So I would advise picking your steps with some caution when following this trail. The seasoned Appalachian Trail hikers along here all carry pencil-thick ski poles and are therefore able to avoid smacking the hard ground the way I did. Fortunately it was only painful and not disabling, and I was not forced to spend the night alone in hypothermia country.*
>
> *When I related this downfall to my Aunt Ruth, a former English teacher who hates surprises, she responded, "Do your readers know your book was written by a lunatic?" I assured her that they probably had already surmised as much.*

OVERSTREET CREEK

Stream Type Freestone

Maps USGS Roanoke; DeLorme 43

Access At Blue Ridge Parkway milepost 81, there is a small meadow on the eastern side of the road. Barely visible at the northern end of the meadow is

VA(s) 765, which heads east toward the town of Bedford. Unless you look very sharp, you will miss the road, which is hidden by meadow grass until you are right on top of it. There is no road sign. Follow this steep, winding gravel road for 0.75 mile, until the stream is visible to your right. For the next mile there are numerous accesses to the lower end.

As you follow the steep gravel road downward, the first hint of the stream is a spout of water shooting out of the bank above the roadway. Farther down it becomes a branch, and a couple of tributaries later it grows into Overstreet Creek, a stream just large enough to hold native trout. Flowing through an abandoned apple orchard, which is part of Jefferson National Forest, the stream is surrounded by thick brambles and brush.

Downstream, just before you enter posted land, access can be had through a couple of paths, crossing the remains of old stone walls. From there, about half a mile upstream, there are decent-sized plunge pools holding some very shy, small brookies.

During the late summer and early fall, an Adams number 16 has proven effective. If that doesn't work, the same-sized Hare's Ear nymph taken to the bottom by tumbling rapids may reach the trout holding as deep as they can to escape the August or September heat.

Overstreet Creek is not for everyone, but the true lover of small native streams will find a pleasurable half day's fishing there. A 6-foot wand of a graphite rod with number 4 line and a 7X tippet have proven effective. Because it's only 40 miles north of Roanoke, located close to the road, this water is accessible—maybe even too accessible—for a couple of hours' diversion before an Indian-summer sunset.

You don't have to be an arch-conservationist to look at one of the little orange-bellied residents of Overstreet Creek and realize that it shouldn't be killed. There are plenty of aquatic insects here, and a busy population of black and red ants. At this writing there is no evidence of acid pollution. Treated gently, the native population can continue to furnish enjoyment for future generations.

SHOOTING CREEK

Stream Type Freestone

Maps USGS Endicott; DeLorme 26

Access Just south of milepost 159 turn left onto VA(s) 860. This is a narrow road, but the roughly 6-mile stretch paralleling Shooting Creek is paved all the way to VA 40. The stream curves away from the road at this lower point and would take some bushwhacking to reach.

Shooting Creek presents the same challenges as other small Blue Ridge Parkway streams. Although not on federal land, it is most conveniently reached from the parkway. Trout are not highly abundant here, and although it was once a stocked stream it is no longer on the state's schedule. There does not appear to have been any specific reason for eliminating it, according to local state freshwater authorities; Shooting Creek seems simply to have just faded from the stocking truck's route.

The stream courses through private land exclusively. Only one section appears to be posted, but the usual courtesy of asking landowners whenever possible is still a good idea. No one resides on the upper stretch, and all that remains of a once active mountain community is a series of half-hidden crumbling chimneys and an occasional graying wooden farmhouse.

Several explanations of Shooting Creek's name have been given. One lady who was born around there charitably believes it derives from the water "shooting" down the mountain through the boulders. There has also been at least one notorious shooting, of a farm wife in her home. Perhaps the most believable explanation came from a conversation with a resident in the local general store. "During Prohibition, folks up Shooting Creek would perch in the boulders. Any strangers coming up the road would be greeted with a barrage of squirrel rifle fire."

That sort of danger is history now. A new generation of more friendly residents has moved in along the lower stretch toward VA 40. There is one other hazard here, however, perhaps because of the number of old deserted houses. A talented lady fly-tier who lives nearby and fishes the stream frequently says that in midsummer copperheads may be seen on the road in considerable numbers.

Around 2.5 miles below the parkway, the origin of Shooting Creek is first glimpsed. It's only a small rivulet trickling around Turner's Knob. Trees blasted by the ice storms of 1994 almost hide the water along some stretches. Farther downstream there are fewer blowdowns, but the banks are thickly overgrown with spicewood, ironwood, and other woody brush. Even roll-casting is a challenge, not made any easier by the numerous twigs snagging your fly under the surface. This is not a stream for the impatient.

There is a fair amount of aquatic life present, with small, sporadic midge hatches in May and later. The minnow population appears healthy. But the livelihood of these hardy wild rainbows is the terrestrial population dropping from the bushes. Number 22 black ants and Crowe Beetles have been moderately effective. The lower half of Shooting Creek is silting over somewhat, and the upper stretch seems to be retaining the best trout population.

Five miles down from the parkway there is a logging road that fords the stream. This is a logical entry point, leading to a surprisingly large pool of flat water even allowing for backcasts. A mile farther upstream there is an iron pipe gate just below the road, with a dirt road that fords the stream. On the far bank is a sizable deserted wood farmhouse with a stacked-stone foundation. It has been reported that the feeding stations upstream from this point are moderately productive.

ROCK CASTLE CREEK (HEADWATERS)

Stream Type Freestone

Maps USGS Woolwine; DeLorme 25

Access Just before milepost 170, turn east at the sign that reads ROCKY KNOB and keep following the signs leading down to the Rocky Knob cabins. Just before reaching the camping area, park at the head of the Rocky Knob Gorge hiking trail. Follow this down the mountain for approximately 1.5 miles, or until fishable water is reached.

During the winter of 1993–94, this area experienced the most severe ice storm in 80 years. There are extensive blowdowns across the trail—not just tree trunks, but the entire tops of trees with a tangle of limbs. These will probably be there for years to come, and enough hiking time should be allowed for skirting around obstacles left by the storm.

Most maps show this stream originating alongside VA 8 far down in the valley. Like many Blue Ridge Parkway streams coming down off the crest, it's unmapped and somewhat obscure, looking more like boggy streaks crisscrossing Rocky Knob Gorge trail. As you follow the trail downward, however, after a mile or so there's a respectable gurgle alongside you. This is the infant Rock Castle Creek beginning to form up some miniature plunge pools and undercut banks. If you continue, there's a sandy flat where the shadows of brook trout scurry from under the rhododendron.

This one is strictly for the true aficionado of small-stream fishing. The brookies are tiny, for the most part under 7 inches. Any movement looks to them like a mink or heron about to have them for lunch, so extreme caution is necessary. Although to my knowledge no specific trout-stalking camouflage has yet hit the market, this would be an ideal place to test it out. Overhanging brush makes backcasts a nightmare.

But the upper reach of Rock Castle has less tangible rewards. After untangling your number 22 terrestrials from the hemlock branches, watching the little flashes of color dart from beneath your feet, and maybe catching two or three of them between hangs, you look up at your surroundings. If it's mid-May, you will see cascades of red trillium assaulting either side of the trail. If it's January, you will see, off among the bare tree trunks, the stone chimneys and thresholds of a mountain community that once thrived

The author prepares to hike down Rocky Knob Trail from the Blue Ridge Parkway to Rock Castle Creek headwaters.

here. Rarely will you see another fisherman in this gorge, because of the difficulty of hiking in and then back out, up the mountain to the top of Rocky Knob. Most stream-lashers would prefer to park along VA 8, step out of their vehicles, and begin casting for stocked trout in the lower part of this stream. Fishing the parkway Rock Castle is a somewhat different experience.

Like the gradient on most of these small headwaters, Rock Castle's pitch is too steep to allow the calm water necessary for hatches of any size. There are abundant minnows here, so small streamers are recommended during the winter months. During warm weather red and black ants as well as the smaller beetle ties work as well as any terrestrials. But it pays to check the banks to see what is crawling or find out what's dropping from the tips of overhanging limbs.

9 | Virginia's Pay-for-Fish Trout Streams

Most of my research on the following private streams was done during February and March, due to scheduling requirements. Because of the fickle nature of southwest Virginia winters, some days were spent in shirtsleeves, following blue-winged olive and midge hatches. But one memorable day I slid through the snow into the 37-degree waters of Escatawba's Dunlap Creek. For anyone interested, felt soles were not designed for snow. Each time I walked the bank I picked up a 3-inch clog of hard-packed white stuff. Despite the wintry landscape, a couple of 2-pound rainbows took my Brown Glitter streamer.

Overall, Virginia winter fishing proved most rewarding. Due to the productivity of these pay-for-fish streams, I caught more huge rebel rainbows than ever before in my life. The spring creeks maintained a moderate water temperature range, and there were plenty of nymphs beneath the limestone rocks. The fish are tail-walking lively in their spawning colors during nippy weather. And best of all, there are usually no other fishermen in sight. Vermont stream-lashers may consider a winter migration to Virginia while their trout waters are ice-locked. Virginia's pay-for-fish network has prompted some to make a vacation circuit of several private streams. I asked one owner, Derrick Barr, where he saw this trend going.

"I'd like to see this become an even higher-quality fishery, with super-large trout. I want people to have an enjoyable experience here, and not only from hooking dozens of fish. I'd like to think a fisherman will bring his family along, and they can hike, take wildlife photographs, wade the stream, swim, or just sit back and enjoy the scenery." His operation, Escatawba, is a little piece of mountain paradise, typical of the best pay-for-fish endeavors. It pays for owners such as Derrick Barr to preserve this pristine look, manage the trout habitat well, and make fishing as close to a wilderness experience as possible.

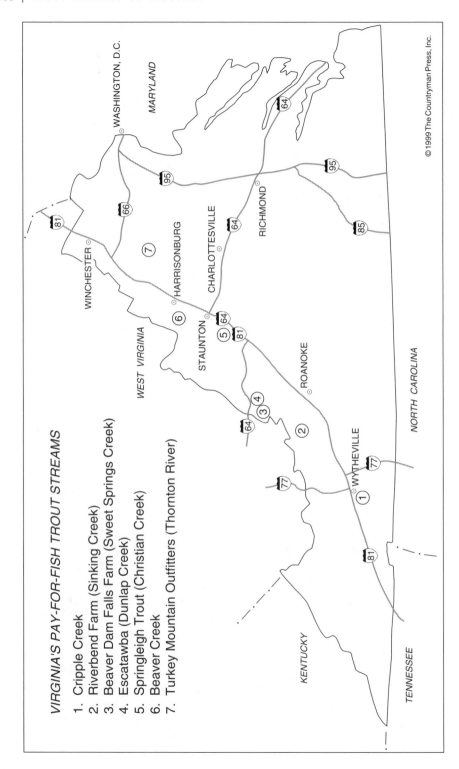

VIRGINIA'S PAY-FOR-FISH TROUT STREAMS

1. Cripple Creek
2. Riverbend Farm (Sinking Creek)
3. Beaver Dam Falls Farm (Sweet Springs Creek)
4. Escatawba (Dunlap Creek)
5. Springleigh Trout (Christian Creek)
6. Beaver Creek
7. Turkey Mountain Outfitters (Thornton River)

He added, "I believe the future of trout fishing in Virginia lies with the young people. We have to find a way to reach this new generation and alert them to outdoor pleasures. That's why I keep a couple of ponds loaded with big trout—so the kids can hook into a 5-pound rainbow. A 10-year-old boy came here. He'd always been a spin-fisherman. I put a fly-rod in his hand, taught him how to use it, and after 20 casts he caught a fish. He was thrilled."

Southwest Virginia is a land of small farmers for whom making a profit has become difficult. Many are making an economy-to-scale decision, selling off their cattle and land, turning green country into housing developments. With so little traditional agricultural income available, trout farming is becoming an attractive alternative. There is a wealth of trout fishermen in Virginia, and also a wealth of small streamside farms. It's only natural that there should be a burgeoning of pay-for-fish operations. In fact, Virginia Tech University has issued a study on the feasibility of trout farming.

Not everyone agrees that private trout preserves are a good thing. One knowledgeable trout conservationist, whose opinion I normally value, had this to say: "I think that the proliferation of pay-for-fish streams is bad overall. It slowly moves us in the direction of the landed gentry being the only ones who will eventually have access or be able to pay to fish. This is not England! It may have a side benefit of keeping some areas from being converted to development or subdivided for other uses. But what good is a resource if you don't have access to it? It is true that wildlife/environmental resources are inherently valuable. That is to say there is an intangible value associated with the fact that these resources exist for their own sake or value. The problem is, how do we as a society maintain a connection with the natural environment and the understanding and appreciation of that environment if we are cut off from it more and more?"

The fact is that Virginia stream owners are closing down public access, and consequently closing down trout stocking, on mile after mile of their trout water. Why is this happening? Is it because owners are valuing their privacy more than in previous decades? Or is it because some irresponsible fishermen, leaving empty beer cases, have angered owners and brought out the POSTED signs? Perhaps it's both. The Virginia Department of Game and Inland Fisheries does the best job possible to please trout license buyers. It is constantly on the lookout for new streams that may be opened to the public. But in spite of its efforts, public trout access is shrinking. At the same time, trout fishing as a sport in Virginia is growing by rainbow leaps. This has resulted in squeezing more anglers into formerly solitary streams. One of my readers from New York came to Virginia for wilderness fly-fishing, hiked 2.5 miles down Bearwallow Run Trail through a wilderness area, and instead of the solitude he was seeking, found himself in a crowd on the banks of Laurel Fork. Adding to his frustration, the banks were littered with soda cans and other trash.

Most pay-for-fish operators keep their fishing areas pristinely clean, so people will return. They guarantee privacy by limiting the number of rods on their stream to the point that rarely is anyone else in sight. There is a pretty large contingent of anglers who are looking for fly-fishing-only, with the solitude that allows them to enjoy nature without being elbowed and without tripping over Styrofoam cups. The evidence lies in the full reservation schedule of places like Beaver Dam Falls and Escatawba. They are booked up for weeks ahead. So an overwhelming demand exists and is starting to be met. Just about every month I get a call about another private pay-for-fish operation starting up.

My criterion for selecting streams for the following section was simple. I required a legitimate fly-fishing experience, with no netfuls of trout being dumped in front of me. My research on the best of the pay-for-fish circuit provided really big, healthy trout; peaceful, private surroundings; and the friendship of the many good people who manage these streams.

CRIPPLE CREEK

Stream Type Limestone spring creek

Maps USGS Cedar Springs; DeLorme 23

Number of Rods 25

Usage Fee $25 per rod per day

For Information and Reservations

> Jim Hilton
> Route 1, Box 293-A
> Rural Retreat, VA 24368
> *Phone:* 276-686-4505

Lodging Cedar Springs Lodge at Cripple Creek accommodates 12. For reservations, call 540-696-4505.

Directions The lodge is located 20 minutes off I-81. Take old exit 60, follow VA 749 through Rural Retreat, and go 4 miles beyond Cedar Springs.

I asked Jim Hilton why he opened the Cripple Creek private fishery. His answer was, "To have a place where, for a reasonable fee, the average guy can come and duel with truly large trout, perhaps even the fish of a lifetime." And Virginians can do this without traveling to New Mexico or Wyoming or Alaska.

The key word here is *large,* and maybe even *huge.* Jim inherited the hatchery from his father over 30 years ago and had an even larger vision of where the property should go. And he is one of those energetic people with enough drive to carry out his vision to the letter. Not large himself, he still looks trim enough to go 10 rounds in an amateur lightweight prize ring. The word *huge* applies to the trout. There are some 8- to 10-pounders lurking under the banks, and Jim says, "Some mornings the leaders breaking out here sound like rifle shots!" The reel drag is a necessity, and it's a good idea to check your line for cuts or abrasions. Also rewind your line, as it's sure to break if it seizes up when one of these animated logs starts its run. On some days the trout won't touch a heavier tippet. So you drop down to a 4-pound test, and what happens? A 5-pound rainbow streaks from behind a log, strips off your line, and pops the tippet!

After being told that brook trout were a difficult, slow-growing species, Jim introduced brook trout into his hatchery. They were anything but slow-growing. In one year Cripple Creek recorded 625 citation brook trout, with equally impressive numbers on rainbows and browns. In 1999 Cripple Creek once again led the state in citations with a total of 356, of which 253 were for brook trout at least 16 inches and weighing over 2 pounds. That's a lot of monster trout. One brookie weighed 6 pounds, 5 ounces and would have broken existing state records except for one technicality. Before it could be verified by a state fisheries biologist, the angler ate his fish!

This plethora of hefty fish is no accident, but the result of a thoughtful hatchery program. It's run by Jim and his wife, Carlene, their nephew Randy Hilton, plus another partner, Jim Trivette. They raise all their own trout from scratch, in a hatchery that looks as sparkling clean as a four-star restaurant's kitchen. This ensures the quality of fish and keeps the guests' cost low at $25 a day with a limit of five trout. Each morning trout are stocked according to the number of rods on the stream that day. The smallest fish placed are 2-pound brook trout, along with some rainbows running 5 pounds or better. That's why on some spring mornings there's a line waiting at the gate at 6:30 for the stream to open at its assigned time of 7:30. It's the lure of having one of these big-shouldered salmonids slam into your Woolly Bugger.

My first trip to Cripple Creek was during the afternoon, just in time to see strings of citation rainbows and golden trout being trundled up the hill. According to Jim, many people vow to catch and release, but when they finally beach that 5-pounder, they're reluctant to give it up. He estimates that 70 percent of his guests keep their catch. The rest of that day I proceeded to cast magnificently, without catching a single trout. I was relieved to hear that this often happens, as these are anything but pond-raised pushovers, and after a morning of heavy pressure they become even more wily. At least that was my alibi. I have since returned and made an arm-wearying correction to that initial dry haul.

Scenery such as this makes concentration difficult.

I have observed a cross section of anglers on Cripple Creek, everything from wormers seated in folding steel chairs to spin-fishermen scoring with their Mepps to a few "long-rodder" fly-fishers like myself. I used a number 12 black Woolly Bugger with a split shot, following Jim Hilton's recommendation. I also tried some big streamers, like the Rabbit Zonker, some other crayfish imitations, and a variety of nymphs. It was February, so I didn't see any hatches, but I'm told small mayflies and caddis have been known to tempt these fussy fish. And if that doesn't work, midges may bring up some of those extra-wary ones.

Most of the stream flows through meadow, with a variety of lies including undercut banks, underwater logs, rocks, tree roots, and likely-looking feeding stations in pocket water. A small tributary, Blue Spring Creek, has a goodly share of overhanging canopy, and casting must be judicious. There are big fish here also. Only five rods are allowed, guaranteeing plenty of fishing room.

If you want to make a party of it, there's a comfortable lodge at streamside that can accommodate 12. An overnight stay costs $113, including the fishing fee. Weekend rates begin at $350, and there's a grill for cooking your own trout dinner. The advantage is being able to roll out of your queen-sized bed at dawn and begin fishing at 7:30. Or you may wish to stay on the stream until the cutoff at 7 PM and then spend a restful evening in the lodge.

RIVERBEND FARM (SINKING CREEK)

Stream Type Freestone

Maps USGS Newport; DeLorme 41

Number of Rods 4

Usage Fee $40 per rod

Information and Reservations

> Ray Collins
> Riverbend Farm Bed & Breakfast
> 225 Zells Mill Road
> Newport, VA 24128
> *Phone:* 540-544-7849
> *E-mail:* stay@riverbendfarm.com

Lodging On-site bed and breakfast.

Directions From Blacksburg, take VA 460 west to VA 42. Follow VA 42 east approximately 2 miles. Turn left onto Clover Hollow Road (VA 601) and take it for 1 mile. Turn left onto Zells Mill Road (VA 604), and go to the second driveway, where you'll see the RIVERBEND FARM sign over a gate.

The RIVERBEND FARM sign could have been somewhere in Colorado or New Mexico. Driving up to the impressive cedar-and-stone home of Ray and Betty Collins, the western feel was heightened. Ray waved from the porch and welcomed me and my two female fishing companions with the hospitality that has given his place the reputation of a comfortable destination for fly-fishermen and -women. But what struck me was the sight of one of my favorite streams, Sinking Creek, flowing in a graceful arc beyond the lodge.

This is a totally different fishery from the public access upstream (page 135). Those two fly-fishing-only sections flow over a relatively steep gradient, with only a few deeper spots. Here at Riverbend the current has carved out one deep green pool after another against the mountainside, and even from a distance I could see swirls from big fins on their surface. Ray Collins stocks rainbows, browns, and brookies once a month, weather permitting. The catch-and-release rule has allowed them to reach rod-straining size. I was a little skeptical when I heard that his property included only half a mile of stream. But any doubts I may have had were quickly laid to rest by the big-water action.

Starting at the downstream boundary, I tested the water beneath falls formed by a huge downed sycamore that had dropped across the stream. Then, working my way upstream, I began to realize that there are times when half a mile of stream is more than enough. My thoughts were interrupted by a gargantuan strike, which broke my 6X tippet and left me one

Woolly Bugger short. Changing to a 4X, I was able to hold the next series of rainbow assaults that severely tested my St. Croix 4-weight pack rod.

I was pleased to see that one of my fishing companions, Katharyn Douglass Hopkins, was having the same sort of success, beaching the largest fish of the day, a respectable 19-inch rainbow. Betty Collins, my other companion, kept a watchful eye on her release technique, making sure a Collins pet fish wasn't stressed out.

I spent most of the day fishing Riverbend, going back and reworking the 60-foot-wide holes. Although comfortable in hippers this February day, I had a feeling that chest waders would be needed with the spring rains. On the other hand, a novice could get plenty of fly-casting from the well-manicured bank.

This would be an ideal location for a family to start up its stream-lashing career. Ray Collins runs a hands-on fly-fishing class, which lasts 3 days and includes lodging and meals for $695 per student. Not a bad anniversary present for a wife who may be envious of her trout-fanatic husband's hobby. Ray puts great emphasis on teaching the sport and confesses to taking it too seriously sometimes, spending a great deal of his time at the fly-tying bench.

Ray has a keen eye for hatches, with a fly-tying bench 30 seconds away from the stream. The emergences he has observed at Riverbend are:

- **Spring** Quill gordons, blue quills, hendricksons, caddis
- **Summer** Green drakes, pale evening duns, light cahills, mahogany duns, little yellow stoneflies, caddis
- **Fall** Little black stoneflies, caddis

Some of most effective flies are those matching the above hatches, but the below-listed nymphs, streamers, and terrestrials predominate when hatches are lacking:

- **Drys** Elk Hair Caddis, Parachute Adams, Sulphurs
- **Nymphs** Bead-Head Princes, Bead-Head Hare's Ears
- **Streamers and Terrestrials** Muddler Minnows, Woolly Buggers, Crystal Buggers, Japanese beetles, black beetles, ants (black and rust), hoppers

Sinking Creek has been one of my favorites for many years. Fishing Riverbend and sampling the hospitality of Ray and Betty Collins added a new and colorful dimension to my old stream-lashing haunt.

ESCATAWBA (DUNLAP CREEK)

Stream Type Freestone, spring-fed

Maps USGS Callaghan; DeLorme 52

Number of Rods 8

Usage Fee $50 per rod per day

Casting amid the clear-running waters of Dunlap Creek.

For Information and Reservations

Escatawba Farms
c/o Derrick E. Barr
P.O. Box 270
Dunlap Creek Road
Covington, VA 24426
Office: 540-962-6487
Home: 540-965-8577; 540-962-5857

Lodging Old Earlhurst Bed & Breakfast (12 miles south); call 540-559-3071.

Directions From Roanoke take I-81 north to VA 220. Go north on VA 220 to I-64 at Clifton Forge. Take I-64 past Covington to exit 10. Turn left (west) onto US 60. After half a mile turn onto VA 159 south at the junction. Take VA 159 for 5 miles to the farm and office on the right.

For a scenic drive from Roanoke, take VA 311 at Hanging Rock. Follow it over three mountains to the intersection with VA 159 in the town of Crows. Turn onto VA 159 and go 5 miles, until you reach Escatawba on the left.

Driving past Sweet Chalybeate, I wondered why the label *Little Montana* had been tagged to this Escatawba stretch of Dunlap Creek, toward which I was headed. Wading into its distilled-clear water, I glanced up and saw part of the answer. The steep upthrust of Sweet Springs Mountain carried a heavy overgrowth of white pine and hemlock, spanning the slope to streamside. Then as my felt soles slid down the shank of a sharp-angled boulder, I saw the bottom strewn with craggy western-style stones scattered like the irregular blocks of some giant's petulant child. Two slippery rocks later I found myself waist-deep in the Dunlap with a hard-fighting Shasta strain rainbow testing my rod.

Escatawba, a Shawnee word meaning "clear-running water," is an apt name for this stretch of the Dunlap. Five evenly spaced springs feed Derrick Barr's private pay-for-fish stretch. The headwaters are Sweet Springs Run, Cove Creek, and Sweet Chalyshea, which coalesce into the Dunlap from the north. Just south are two good native brook trout streams, Crose Run and Little Crose Run.

A hundred years ago all of the outpouring of mountain aquifers made this area a choice destination for spa-bound tourists. Today Escatawba attracts fly-anglers looking for the thrill of tying into big rainbows—some in the 5-pound range. Its spring-fed rush delivers 700 gallons of calcium-rich water per minute, with temperatures ranging from 42 degrees in February and March to just over 70 in August.

One unforgettable early-March day, I skidded through a snowbank into the depths of the Dunlap and glanced up at the overhanging mountain. The dusting of snow on every needle of the trees could have been sparkling on a Sangre de Cristo spur of the Rockies. On this snowmelt day the temperature hovered around 37 degrees—definitely not hatch weather, even for blue-winged olives. It was a day to put the "meat" on: Woolly Buggers, Peach Glitter streamers, Muddler Minnows, and an assortment of nymphs. This was not a typical day on the Dunlap, when as many as 50 heavy-hitting rainbows can leave you arm-weary at the end of a day. The rapids weren't producing, but finally in the flats, where the current slowed enough to warm, a couple of 2-pounders ran with my streamer. It took some split shot, bouncing along the bottom, to overcome that day's challenge. A huge grab stiffened my line and quickly broke my 3-weight tippet. This was the action I had heard about: 24-inch trout. Derrick Barr has been stocking the creek for 18 years, but 1999 was the first year it was opened to the public. Somewhere in the deep holes are veteran holdovers no one has yet been able to roll to the surface. It's anybody's guess how big they really are.

The hatches anticipated here in the freestone will be somewhat different from those found in the upper tributaries, which are limestone. Quill gordons and march browns are a good early-spring bet. With all of its deep pools, Escatawba is a nymphing paradise, and a weighted Prince bounced along the bottom is almost sure to get attention year-round.

SPRINGLEIGH TROUT (CHRISTIAN CREEK)

Stream Type Limestone spring creek

Maps USGS Verona; DeLorme 66

Number of Rods 6

Usage Fee $40 full day, $30 half day (4 hours)

Information and Reservations

> H. Joseph Williams Jr.
> Springleigh Trout
> Route 1, Box 556
> Greenville, VA 24440
> *Phone:* 540-337-3451
> *E-mail:* Springleightrout@Juno.com

Directions Nine miles south of Staunton, take exit 213 to VA 11. Turn north for 0.5 mile, then left onto VA 701. Go 1 mile to the second left onto VA 604, then 1 mile to the first right onto VA 817. Follow VA 817 for 0.75 mile to the first entrance on the left. Springleigh is 1¾ hours west of Richmond and 1½ hours north of Roanoke.

Driving over the bridge into Springleigh Trout, it struck me that this place was made for small-stream connoisseurs. Christian Creek is jump-across width as it winds downstream through a herd of browsing cattle. The vista upstream was somewhat more encouraging, with gentle rapids dropping into decent-sized pools, overhung with enough vegetation to provide cooling shade in summer.

This was February, so nymphs were the order of the day. Tying on a Bead-Head Flashback Hare's Ear, I laid it beneath the overhanging grass. The Kamloops rainbows in Christian Creek lie under the banks, and here's a challenge. It takes perfect placement of the fly—not in the grass, not in midstream, but within a 5-inch circle at the undercut where the fish are hiding. The nymph drifted into the feeding pattern of a patriarch rainbow and the fight was on.

Upstream the thick brush devoured a hefty population out of my flybox. Rather than casting I began to flip the line 8 feet or less in some spots, and dap between the branches in others. The trout splashed up virtually between my feet and this pattern repeated itself, with strong fish streaking back and forth in that tiny stream, breaking tippets about a third of the time. There are rainbows and brook trout here up to 20 inches. Owner Joe Williams also stocks browns and golden trout, and there are even a few native brookies flourishing. One reason these fish are so vibrant is the 2,000-gallons-per-minute flow from the two springs that give birth to

Dapping the Springleigh.

Christian Creek. Add to that the rich food supply from the limestone bed, and you get healthy fish. Joe actually raises trout in his stream with as much success as in runways or ponds.

Spring hatches are the usual march browns and sulphurs, with brown caddis predominating among summer species. The lower meadows are a rich source of beetles, ants, hoppers, crickets, and assorted leaf eaters. It pays to carefully study this 1.5-mile insect microcosm to see what terrestrials are dropping from the overhanging grass, the color and size of nymphs under rocks, and whether the ever-present blue-winged olives are hatching. Springleigh is the kind of place that makes a slow, careful, magnifying-glass approach rewarding.

Joe Williams features himself as a trout culturist with a conservative conservationist's, rather than a strict preservationist's, outlook. He believes in a balanced environment with thoughtful harvesting of resources. It's catch-and-release only, with wading discouraged, although I found neoprene a help in marshy spots.

Toward the end of the Springleigh day I broke the upstream rule and began drifting a black Woolly Bugger downstream, trailing it into the under-cuts. This lured some great thrashing rainbows from their lairs. It also cut down on the number of flies I left snagged in the alder bushes. I left Springleigh with this thought: Think small stream, but large trout.

BEAVER CREEK

Stream Type Limestone

Maps USGS Verona; DeLorme 66

Special Regulations Single-hook, fly-fishing only, catch-and-release.

Number of Rods 4

Information and Reservations Four $5.00 passes per day are issued at Billy's Blue Ridge Angler fly-shop in Harrisonburg and at the Mossy Creek fly-shop. It's a good idea to call ahead and reserve your place on the stream. For information and reservations, contact:

Billy Kingsley
1887 South Main Street
Harrisonburg, VA 22801
540-574-3474

Lodging Boxwood Bed and Breakfast; call 540-867-5772.

Directions To reach Billy Kingsley's Blue Ridge Angler shop, take exit 245 (Harrisonburg) off I-81. Drive west on Port Republic Road (VA 241) to VA 11. Go south on VA 11 for 1.2 miles, and Billy's shop is on the right. Once you have your orange permit, drive down VA 11 to the first stoplight and turn right on Mosby Road. Then turn left onto VA 42 and immediately bear right on VA 257. Follow VA 257 for about 7 miles, across the Dry River, to where it turns sharply to the left. Go straight onto VA 742. You'll see the Ottobine Elementary School on your right, and parking for fly-fishers is restricted to the school parking lot. Just across the road is Beaver Creek, with a world of great rainbow fishing.

March came in like a lamb on Beaver Creek, just south of Harrisonburg. It was a shirtsleeve 60 degrees, and Trico and midge hatches were swarming as my companion and I high-stepped the four turnstiles en route downstream. Katharyn Douglass Hopkins, a veterinary surgeon occasionally known as Katydid, was entrusted to me by her mother for a day's fly-fishing. She is an accomplished fly-fisher, totally focused, and her only flaw is a tendency to occasionally outfish me. Reaching the lower boundary of the Beaver, Douglass tied on a Prince, and on her fourth cast landed a healthy 12-inch brown. "Man," I thought, "this is going to be a gold-medal day."

Beaver Creek is a mile stretch of limestone creek managed by Billy Kingsley, the Massanutten chapter of Trout Unlimited, and landowners in a unique cooperative. Billy Kingsley requests a contribution of no more than $5.00 per person, which is used for stream maintenance and stocking. The landowners are enthusiastic participants in this workable plan, and even ask fly-fishers to show their passes. Hopefully the Beaver can serve as a model

Hooking a rainbow with the Beaver Creek Special.

for other streams and other TU chapters.

Billy laid a stream map on the table and with a yellow highlighter scribed the upper quarter mile of the Beaver around the access bridge. "This section has been pretty heavily hit, so you may wish to fish farther downstream." That fit in with our plans, as I wanted to cover the entire regulated stretch. So that's how it happened that Douglass hooked her initial brown at the VA 257 highway bridge, which is the downstream boundary.

One negative was the great blue heron we scared up. As it flapped its huge wings and sailed away, I had the feeling that the trout crowd had taken cover. This downstream section had a lot of flat, clear water, but in spite of the good visibility, we couldn't see any fish in the water, which may have been because of the big bird.

There followed a 2-hour trout moratorium with no hookups or strikes.

We fished the 20-minute rule upstream, changing nymphs at least three times per hour, and—nothing. Bead-Head Hare's Ears, Woolly Worms, Woolly Buggers, Crowe Beetles, Rabbit Zonkers, Muddler Minnows—all were totally ignored by Beaver Creek salmonids. Turning over rocks, I uncovered a very pale green aquatic crawly and searched my fly-box for something to imitate it. The closest I could find was a little Olive Quill nymph, tied much too bright a green. As I anticipated, they wouldn't touch it.

After a lunch break we drove back to the Blue Ridge Angler and confronted Billy Kingsley. "What do we need, Billy?" I asked.

A little reluctantly, I thought, he reached into his fly bin and produced an ungainly little nymph. It was a neutral buff-colored number 16 with a scruffy tuft of iridescent green sticking out of the tip, looking for all the world like a miniature sea cucumber. "This will work," he assured us. "It looks a little drab, but that neutral body takes on the color of the water." Looking at it I could see that it was exactly like the pale green crawly I had seen on that overturned rock. Now it was time to get back to the Beaver and get down to business. On Beaver Creek, this day the color was green.

Right away I hooked into a heavy 14-inch rainbow with that new nymph. Excited, I looked for Douglass, who had the camera around her neck, and I could see her head just over the bank several hundred yards away. Hanging on to the fish, I whistled my best for several minutes, until finally she turned her head and trotted over for the photo.

"I heard you whistling but thought it was a bird," she said.

I then caught a smaller rainbow and held it up for a picture. "Make it look as big as possible. I'm holding it up against my red shirt."

"You're holding it against your stomach. How can I make it look big by comparison?" asked Douglass.

"Okay, okay, just take the picture."

Billy's Beaver Creek Special worked well for us the rest of the afternoon, snagging rainbows a couple of hundred yards below the access bridge and just below the dam upstream. Above the dam is a small impoundment with a large sycamore tree overhanging it. Fish were surfacing just under a sycamore limb, obviously on some sort of tiny terrestrial. Douglass tried a number of imitations, but without any luck, as these fish are very picky, in spite of being stocked. Without exactly the right pattern, they just won't respond.

We had anticipated a couple of hours' worth of fishing, but this stream afforded a delightful full day of stream-lashing. In fact, the time caught up with us, and it was dusk by the time we left. If you like meadow streams with plenty of holdover rainbows and browns, the Beaver is your ticket.

TURKEY MOUNTAIN OUTFITTERS (THORNTON RIVER)

Stream Type Freestone

Maps USGS Washington; DeLorme 74

Number of Rods 4

Usage Fee Nonguided: $50 half day, $85 full day. Guided, $75 half day, $140 full day, includes flies and lunch. It is recommended that you hire a guide on your first visit to Turkey Mountain, as there are specific ledges under which larger fish lurk.

For Information and Reservations

Jim and Jenny Hickey
P.O. Box 241
Sperryville, VA 22740
Phone: 540-987-9134
Fax: 540-987-7233

Directions From northern Virginia and Washington, DC, take I-66 west to Gainesville. From Gainesville take VA 29 south to Warrenton and then VA 211 west almost to Sperryville. Turkey Mountain Outfitters is headquartered on Mount Vernon Farm, off VA 211 east toward Warrenton (0.5 mile northwest of Sperryville, Virginia).

From Richmond, take I-64 west to the Gordonsville exit. Follow VA 15 north to Gordonsville, then take VA 231 to Madison and on to Sperryville. In Sperryville turn right on VA 211 east.

From I-81, exit at New Market and follow VA 211 east through Luray to Sperryville.

Turkey Mountain Outfitters is 2 hours from Richmond, 1 1/2 hours from Washington, DC, 1 1/4 hours from Charlottesville, and 45 minutes from I-81.

Tumbling down from the Shenandoah Range, the South and North Forks of the Thornton River converge just outside of Sperryville, Virginia. Until that confluence, these are typical, hard-running Shenandoah Park brook trout fisheries falling thousands of feet off the summit. At the confluence there is one last spate of rapids, and then the Thornton seems to breathe a sigh of relief and begin a tranquil flow through gentle pastures. The green barn you encounter is home to Turkey Mountain Outfitters. The mountain itself looks more like a hill compared to the towering Shenandoah Range, but it's home to flocks of the big birds, which come down to the river for a drink of water and to peck about the banks.

At this point the Thornton is truly a river, and a horse of a river at that, some 40 to 50 feet across. Chest waders are a must, and the trout are a

Katharyn Douglass Hopkins with her first Turkey Mountain rainbow.

healthy 14 inches and above. The population is largely Kamloops rainbow and brook trout, with no browns for fear that they may migrate into the park and devour the fry of the pure brook strain. Most of the lower Thornton brookies are big stockers, but occasionally the brilliant little park strain invades the private stretch. This usually occurs later in the spring, when they are seeking the coolness of deeper pools.

My first encounter with the lower Thornton was on a windy April day with the water temperature hovering around 51 degrees. The rig suggested by guide Jim Hickey was a number 16 Quill Gordon with a dark Hare's Ear as a dropper tied a couple of feet down. This worked well enough to hook a beauty of a 15-inch holdover brook trout and a couple of somewhat larger rainbows. As I remarked to Jim, we really were nymphing that day, as nothing took a swipe at the Quill Gordon, which served only as a strike indicator.

It was one of those "You shoulda been here three days ago" situations when Jim assured me the dark caddis were swarming. This is a freestone stream, but rather than hard quartzite, the bed is sedimentary, encouraging healthy insect propagation. The crevices are filled with sand and gravel, which form frequent redds and make for easy footing. The evidence of spawning shows up in the 3- and 4-inch fry occasionally hooked.

In addition to the hatches listed below, the overhanging trees and bushes assure ample terrestrials dropping in during the summer. Meadow grass lines the banks on some stretches, supplying a hopper diet in warm weather. Although the pay-for-fish section is closed from June until October, the fish manage to survive the warm weather due to this bountiful terrestrial diet and cooling spring branches that continue to run in summer. There is a stocking in the fall and again in the spring.

Thornton River Hatches include:

- **Spring** Caddis, quill gordons, blue-winged olives, yellow stoneflies, light cahills, march browns, sulphurs
- **Summer** Caddis, green drakes, Tricos
- **Fall** Caddis, Tricos, black stoneflies, blue-winged olives
- **Winter** Caddis, black stoneflies

The most effective attractor flies here include:

- **Nymphs** Bead Head Pheasant Tails, Hare's Ears, Princes
- **Streamers** Woolly Buggers, Muddler Minnows
- **Drys** Royal Wulffs, Stimulators

I recommend the following equipment:

- **Waders** Chest, felt-soled
- **Rod and Line** Medium-action 5-weight with low-visibility floating line; 4X or 5X 9-foot leader; about 5-pound test, depending on the manufacturer

The 2-mile pay-for-fish area is divided into four sections, each with unique characteristics. There is a combination of man-made and natural waterfalls, pocket-water rapids, and many pools up to 8 feet deep. The river increases in size as spring branches feed in. First-time visitors to the Thornton may be expecting tame, pondlike fishing for docile trout. When confronted with the many intricate casting problems, along ledges and under sycamore roots, they scratch their heads in wonder. And the trout are anything but tame. One 17-incher bent my 5-weight Clearwater in ten different directions for 20 minutes and finally wrapped the tippet around a root despite my efforts to flat-bend him away. He left the Quill Gordon neatly embedded in a root, leading me to conclude he had used this escape technique before. He surfaced a couple of times, flashing his brilliant scarlet holdover color, which was reward enough.

My next rainbow turned out to be a leaper, clearing the surface by a couple of feet half a dozen times. It was a thrill to watch, but it necessitated landing the fish after only a couple of minutes, as tail-walking tends to quickly exhaust a fish. My companion, Katharyn Douglass Hopkins, landed a rainbow that she graciously said was no larger than my catches, even though it may have been. As she played the bruiser around a pool, at least a dozen large rainbows came out of hiding to swarm about their hooked companion. It began to look like a saltwater frenzy for a while. Although smarter and more difficult to approach, there are some 4- and 5-pounders here.

My guide for the day was Jim Hickey, although his wife, Jenny, is an equally competent alternative. Together they take parties of no more than four clients to Patagonia during the summer, fishing for the incredible brown trout in the shadow of the Andes. On the Thornton Jim specifies fly-fishing-only, catch-and-release with barbless hooks. The "Outfitters" refers to the rental equipment available at $15 a day, and flies and outfits are also for sale. Jim and Jenny also offer fly-fishing instruction at $20 per hour, $80 for a half day, and $150 for a full day.

ABOUT THE AUTHOR

A native Virginian, Harry Slone recalls his first encounter with angling in the state's gemlike streams. At age seven, he was hoisted onto the shoulders of an unreconstructed fly-fisher, who waded into the Blue Hole on the Bullpasture River. That senior stream-lasher then cast his Royal Coachman past the young future author, leaving an indelible memory.

An 18-year residence in Pennsylvania gave Slone another picture of fly-fishing, one rich in tradition and liberally documented. His return to Virginia brought him the idea of at least beginning some documentation of the Old Dominion's trout legacy. This book is the outgrowth of that comparison of Virginia with Pennsylvania.

A freelancer in the medical field, Mr. Slone features himself as "a writer who fly-fishes rather than a fly-fishing authority who writes." He adds that all the observations in this book are the result of personal encounters with all the Virginia trout streams featured. The descriptions are therefore honest impressions of the waters and the fish they contain—maybe not what others would see, but a true delineation of what he saw.

INDEX

Books from The Countryman Press and Backcountry Guides

We offer many more books on hiking, bicycling, canoeing and kayaking, travesl, nature, and country living. Our books are available at bookstores and outdoor stores everywhere. For more information or a free catalog, please call 1-800-245-4151, or write to us at The Countryman Press, P.O. Box 748, Woodstock, Vermont 05091. You can find us on the Internet at www.countrymanpress.com